I0815603

good
news
preaching

Good News Preaching

Offering the Gospel in Every Sermon

Revised with New Sermons

GENNIFER BENJAMIN BROOKS

Revised Foreword by Ronald J. Allen

The Pilgrim Press, 1300 East 9th Street
Cleveland, Ohio 44114
thepilgrimpress.com

Published 2025.

Printed on acid-free paper.

Library of Congress Cataloging-in-Publication Data on file.
LCCN: 2025938957

ISBN (paper): 978-0-8298-0350-1
ISBN (ebook): 978-0-8298-1271-8

Printed in The United States of America.

CONTENTS

foreword

In many ways, the foreword that I wrote for the first edition still fits the situation of the preacher. That foreword began,

> Imagine stepping into the pulpit on Sunday morning or Saturday night and looking into the faces of the congregation. What do you see? An older woman whose husband was interred last month and who is in the grip of grief. A young couple trying to conceive a child. A woman sitting at a strange angle on the pew because her husband hit her again. Three people in their late fifties who work at the local plant whose supervisors told them on Friday that the plant will close in three weeks. A high school student struggling with feelings of attraction toward persons of the same gender. Parents who have a child serving in Iraq for whom every news bulletin is a moment of panic. A lesbian couple who has just been told that their application for adoption has been refused—again. A member is resentful because you did not get to the hospital quickly enough while that person was there. A secret drinker. One member who has been convicted of a crime and is awaiting

> sentencing and another who was surprised at home late at night by an intruder in the bedroom. And this first impression of the congregation does not consider the full range of the news that comes across the television, internet, radio, and newspaper, from violence and poverty and racial/ethnic tensions to environmental catastrophe in so many corners of the world. Preachers ask themselves, "What does such a listener need to hear from my sermon?"

Many of the same people—or others like them—will be in the congregation nearing the end of the first quarter of the twenty-first century. The preacher must still ask, "What do they need from a sermon?" But other factors, while not absent before, had a lower profile but now are in the faces of the congregation. Political partisanship of the most volatile sort is now commonplace. In fact, it is in our eyes and ears from the time we wake up in the morning and connect with the media until we turn off our last device at night—that is, if we ever completely turn off. Not only is political partisanship seemingly ever present but it is expressed in ways that are disrespectful, inflammatory, and sometimes carry the threat of violence. An invitation to dinner at an old friend's house is sometimes an invitation to come and be lobbied. Life, at least as I experience it today, is charged with political tensions that leave my teeth on edge just about all the time. And I never know when something is going to set off a microbomb in my heart and mind.

And there are other sources of anxiety. Every year we learn that planet earth, our island home, is diminishing in its capacity to support humankind and nature. Someone has even coined a word for it—"ecocide," modeled after the word "homicide." How much longer will the earth be able to support the human beings, the animals and the plants and trees that live on it? Although there was a burst of energy to reshape the North American social world in the shape of justice after the killing of George Floyd, that effort has largely dissipated and been replaced by lingering suspicion and even hostility among the races, at least in many places. In a book published in 1903, W. E. B. DuBois famously said that "the problem of race is the problem of the twentieth century." That saying could be adapted to "the problem of race is the problem of the twenty-first century."

For clergy in the long-established denominations, one of the biggest changes that has developed since the first edition is in the church itself. So many congregations are getting smaller. I am frequently a guest preacher in county seat congregations where the attendance used to be about 100 but is now 50, 30, or even smaller. Our denominational structures are correspondingly smaller. In the midst of greater need, we have fewer resources. It can be discouraging. A friend of mine commented, "This is not the church I agreed to serve." And this gives rise to the most existentially gripping question that I asked in the first foreword: Considering your own heart and soul in the early twenty-first century, what do you most need as a preacher? What are the deepest yearnings of your heart, and how can the act of sermon preparation—drawing on the Bible, tradition, experience, and reason—help you as you put together sermons intended to help others?

From my point of view as a professor, as a minister, as a Christian, and as a human being, as the bad spreads and intensifies, so does the need for the approach to preaching that Professor Gennifer Benjamin Brooks sets out in this book. We need good news, empowering news, news that releases us from thinking we are trapped in a world of partisanship and fear and anger and that can move us towards a world of love, justice, peace, respect, and dignity for all. We need to feel that we are a part of a community that reflects the presence and purposes of a liberating and loving God who wants the best for us.

Speaking for myself, having been ordained into the Christian ministry in 1974, I want to feel like I can make a difference. I do not have to think of myself as the leader of a latter-day social revolution, but I would like to think that I can make a difference when I offer myself to become a channel of the Good News about which Brooks speaks so eloquently and powerfully.

The preaching of generations of preachers has been transformed by this book as readers encounter the author's exquisite biblical and theological rationale for why good news should be the basic character of Christian preaching. A preacher floundering in sermon preparation, or an experienced preacher looking for something new, can discover practical guidance in how to identify good news in biblical passages and how to correlate that news with life situations today. The book moves in logical steps from background in preparation to foregrounding the work of shaping the actual sermon so that it becomes an authentic expression of the preacher's understanding and experience of the good news. Think of the preachers as recipients of the good news of which they are speaking!

With the permeating focus on preaching as communicating good, regenerative, restorative news from God, the potential reader might think that Brooks ignores or downplays sin. "What about prophetic challenge?" But this is one of the strengths of the book. Gennifer Benjamin Brooks looks sin and injustice in the eye and names it for what it heinously is and does. The good news has depth and power precisely as it correlates with the depth and power of sin.

Professor Brooks grew up in the Caribbean and spent her early adult life in New York City, where she has been an eyewitness to exploitation, racism, sexism, and violence. She knows the struggle that Christian life can be. This book is no pablum, but rather looks these fierce realities in the eye, and yet it is bold enough to assert that when reality has done its worst, the good news from God is still at work.

No matter how bruised any circumstance may be, God is there in suffering solidarity as well as with an invitation to regeneration. There never is a moment when God is not present. Gennifer Brooks stands on solid exegetical and theological grounds. Hebrew often speaks of good news. For example, in Psalm 68:11, the good news (NRSV: "tidings") is that the enemies of Israel flee as Israel enters the promised land. Psalm 96:2 exults that the good news (NRSV: "tell") is God's salvation, God's reign, which means the possibility of justice and right relationships for all (Psalm 96:10, 13).

In the Torah, Prophets, and Writings, the language of good news reaches its most powerful expression in Isaiah 40–55. The leaders of Israel are in exile. They are discouraged and without hope. To them the prophet says, "Get you up to a high mountain, O Zion, herald of good tidings [good news], lift up your voice with strength . . . lift it up, do not fear; say to the cities of Judah, 'Here is your God!'" The good news is not only that God is present, but that God is at work to release them from exile, to return them home, and to do it all like a shepherd gathering the lambs in his arms (Isaiah 40:9–11; 41:27). This is perhaps the most important part of the Torah, Prophets, and Writings for understanding the good news in the Gospels and Letters.

In an important passage that continues to define the calling of the preacher, Isaiah declares, "How beautiful upon the mountains are the feet of the messenger who announces peace, who brings good news, who announces salvation, who says to Zion, 'Your God reigns'" (52:7; similarly, 60:6; 61:1). The good news is that God, like a monarch, triumphs over the enemies of the welfare of the community.

The Septuagint—the translation of the Hebrew scriptures into Greek and the version of the Gospels, Torah, and Writings that was used by early followers of Jesus—uses the word *euangelion* to speak of the good news. This word is made up of the prefix *eu*, meaning "good," and the noun *angelos*, meaning "news." By definition, then, the gospel is news that has a good quality.

For the apostle Paul, the notion of *euangelion* is so important that he uses it to describe both apostolic vocation and the heart of the apostolic message. Paul is "set apart for the gospel of God" (Romans 1:1). The gospel is "the power of God for salvation" (Romans 1:16–17). For Paul, the good news is that through Jesus Christ, God is ending the present evil age and is leading the world towards an apocalypse (the second coming of Jesus), after which God will remake the cosmos as the divine realm in which all things will take place according to God's purposes. Indeed, when Paul outlines the motives for his own ministry in Romans 10:15, he draws upon Isaiah 52:7.

The first three gospels describe and assert the leading theme of the ministry of Jesus in this way. The first words of Jesus in the Gospel of Mark interpret his entire ministry. "The time is fulfilled, and the realm [NRSV: kingdom] of God has come near; repent and believe in the good news [*evangelion*]" (Mark 1:15). The good news is that God has set in motion the movement towards the eschatological world. Jesus is God's agent in that movement. Matthew uses very much the same language (4:17). Luke introduces the ministry of Jesus with Jesus' sermon in the synagogue at Nazareth in which Jesus quotes from the great Isaiah to explain the Savior's vocation. "The Spirit of [God] is upon me, because [the Spirit] has anointed me to bring good news to the poor" (Luke 4:18; Isaiah 61:1).

Without turning this foreword into an exercise with the concordance, we can see these themes throughout the Gospels and Letters. We find good news as the guiding message in Paul's epistles (for example, Colossians 1:5; Ephesians 3:8; 1 Timothy 1:1; 2 Timothy 1:8). The most fully preserved early Christian sermon, the Letter to the Hebrews, understands the fundamental message to be that of good news (4:2), as do Peter's (1 Peter 1:12) and the final book of the Bible (Revelation 14:6).

The good news from God is good precisely because the bad news of the world is so bad. But no matter whether people regard themselves as stained by their personal sin or crushed by unjust systems, preaching of the kind advocated in this book asserts that God is present not only to comfort and succor but also with liberating intent that seeks to free the oppressed from oppression and the oppressors from their own, different oppression. The journey from a world of bad news to one of good news can be long. It can call for patience and endurance on the part of the preacher. But all along the way, there will be moments when preacher and congregation can catch glimpses of the future already in the present. And even when such glimpses are not in view, there is the reservoir of God's constant presence. We can take this journey in hope because it is a journey towards transformation and regeneration that is beyond our imagining and deeper than our desiring. I know of no better guide on that journey than Professor Gennifer Brooks.

Ronald J. Allen
Professor of Preaching, and Gospels and Letters (Emeritus)
Christian Theological Seminary

introduction

Now ain't that good news.

My greatest desire when I listen to sermons is to be able to say these words when the preacher sits down. Sadly, not only has that not been my response to many of the sermons I've heard over the past few decades, but I have been unable to make that response to a large percentage of the sermons that I have heard since the first publication of this text and in fact for most of my adult life. As I said originally, writing this book was a joyful and challenging experience, and throughout that endeavor, I tried to follow the leading of the Holy Spirit and listen to the whispers of God. The response by clergy and lay persons who have read or studied this text has confirmed for me that what I heard was correct and the book as written fulfilled a need being experienced by many who preached sermons and some who listened to those sermons.

Over the decades of my life that I have spent as an academic, I have been privileged to teach many budding preachers and to share the importance of offering real good news to the listening congregation. I have used this textbook to provide a methodology for framing the good news that speaks of God's active, transformative grace to individuals in the present context and ensuring that the sermon being preached contains recognizable good news. It has been a privilege to know that there are colleagues who use this textbook in their classes for the same reason and that there are individuals, both clergy and laity, who find this text accessible for their own work and their continued development as preachers of the gospel. As I have used this textbook over the past fifteen years, I have added material based on developments in the field of homiletics, and also to address societal issues in the United States and in the world and to call preachers to advance the cause of Christ in the world. As always, I have tried to follow the leading of the Holy Spirit and listen to the whispers of God so that what is offered in the following pages has relevance for the important work of proclamation that is the call of preachers and the nucleus around which the work of ministry is centered.

Preachers and congregations come from different social and cultural locations, and many are located in marginal places. As such they all need to receive good news that tells of God's active presence in their lives and in their situation. That need transcends their physical, spiritual, social, and cultural identities and speaks of the common humanity we share as made in the image of God. The bent to sin that is common to all human beings also makes the need for good news a living reality. Thus, the proclamation of divine grace, realized in the death and resurrection of Jesus Christ and offered freely to all is the bedrock on which the good news stands.

Preaching is the proclamation of the gospel to the people of God in a particular time and place. The word "gospel," translated from a Greek word *evangelion*, meaning good news, implies that the act of preaching is intended to offer good news to the hearers of the preached word. The good news that preaching has to offer even in this postmodern world is the always new thing that God is doing in the redemption of the world through Jesus Christ. Samuel Proctor believes "preaching helps us to find answers to the mystery of human suffering and misfortune,"[1] and that in and of itself is good news. However, in my experience of listening to sermons over the years of my adult life, they too often offer little, if any, good news to the people. Even when the preacher makes the assertion that they are about to name good news, sometimes the good news that is offered is shallow and lacks theological depth. Moreover, too often the so-called good news does not relate in a significant and concrete way to the everyday lives of the congregation.

From the outset, let me state clearly that I am not suggesting that sermons should be all sweetness and light, nor am I advocating the dreaded prosperity gospel that so many in the church find objectionable. To the contrary, I am a strong advocate of presenting a realistic picture of human sinfulness as always needing the redemptive grace of God; but my deep theological conviction is that such presentation should be done only if there is an even stronger offering of divine grace. As was brought home to me in the response to a sermon I preached, if the good news makes living in challenging times seem too easy, it loses authenticity. Nor is it appropriate to simply offer a sinecure for real issues of life by directing the hearers to turn to Jesus. The good news that the sermon offers must be realistic from the standpoint of human possibility even as it rests securely on God's unstinting grace.

Thus, as I thought about what the focus of my first book on preaching would be, I was struck by the need for real sermonic good news. I was influenced also by the challenge such a requirement presents to many of my students and their difficulty or downright inability to discern authentic good news from the biblical text and to offer that good news in their sermons. And as I listened more closely to preachers, even many who are often commended publicly for their preaching, I was struck by how many gave short shrift to offering good news in the construction and delivery of their sermons. And even these many years later since the original publication, sadly, the situation in too many places remains the same. As preachers pivoted in their desire to reach parishioners who could not gather because of COVID-19, and as sermons were offered to or recorded for disembodied congregations, the challenge of offering good news that related to the congregational situation became even more challenging and often downright impossible even for conscientious preachers.

So, the challenge that was put to me some time ago by a preaching student through the question: "Does every sermon need to have explicit good news?" became even more relevant, if such a thing is possible. The budding preacher tried to convince me that good news was automatically present in all sermons because the foundation of Christianity, and therefore of Christian preaching, is the good news of Jesus' redemption of humanity. However, he also presented the argument that there were some sermons in which it was impossible to give good news, perhaps because of a particular biblical text or the context in which the sermon was preached. Of course I continued to disagree with both positions, and affirmed my belief that the sermon offers a definitive and always opportune place for the proclamation of the grace of God.

Good news must be proclaimed clearly because its purpose is to help shape the people of God in their Christian discipleship, and the sermon is the primary vehicle by which the preacher names the good news of God's ongoing act of deliverance. The sermon is a medium by which the preacher offers testimony, and bears witness to the unending presence of the grace of God in scripture, in the world, and in the individual and corporate lives of preacher and congregation. As Ron Allen states, "The sermon is good news not only because it helps the congregation perceive that God is repairing the destructive work of sin, but also because God is constantly in the world to manifest love, justice and other forms of blessing."[2] Thus, the good news of the sermon cannot offer simply a feel-good response to the bad news of human sin; it must reveal God's grace present in the application of the good news to the substance of their lives.

My experience as a discerning listener of sermons began in my troublesome teen years. My pastor, the late Reverend William W. Watty, a leading theologian of Caribbean origin, preached "good" sermons. I could not have told you then what made them good, but on reflection I believe that it was because, first, they did not make me feel chastised even though I was aware of places within myself and actions that I was doing that were less than what was expected of me as an active member of the church. But more than that, they affirmed me as a child of God, one who continued to experience God's love in the midst of evidence that named me, in my mind, as unworthy. And long before I became an elder in the United Methodist Church and accepted my calling as a minister of the Word of God, I was convinced about the need to offer some semblance of good news to hurting people whenever I preached.

Listening to the feedback from congregations I have been privileged to serve solidified in me the belief that as much as the people of God need to confront and admit to their sinfulness, to seek God's justifying grace, and to be challenged to live out their discipleship faithfully, they just as urgently need to hear that they are not alone in their struggles, that God's grace is already theirs and ever available to support their Christian endeavors. As a result, it became a critical element in my preaching that at all times my sermons explicitly offered hearers the good news of God's active, empowering, transforming presence that alone could enable them to fulfill their commitment as disciples of Jesus Christ. My pastoral experiences convinced me that people are hungry for the good news of God's presence with them as they strive to live faithfully as Christians; and those same experiences convinced me of the necessity for every preached sermon to offer recognizable good news.

As a teacher of preaching, it is difficult not to listen to sermons in a regular congregation on a Sunday morning with a critical ear, so I strive intentionally to take off my "professor head" when I attend worship services. What that means is that I refuse to allow myself to evaluate the sermon for form and structure, but I listen intentionally for good news. I do so because I need it as much as every Christian does. In a world that has not only seemingly gone mad in so many ways, but in a country where the divide between groups has been deliberately created and fostered, where the political climate has become toxic, where conflict and separation between racial, cultural, and other iterations of the multi-ethnic, multi-lingual, multi-cultural identities that comprise US society has and continues to widen, the need for sermonic good news is critical. For those who continue to look to the church as that beloved community that followers of Jesus Christ are charged to become, each sermon must be a reminder or, better said, an affirmation, that whatever the trouble we face individually, in society, or in the world, God is still present and active, not only redeeming the world, but also enabling us to live beyond the challenges of our everyday world through that redemptive, transforming, empowering grace. Indeed, the preacher must understand that sermons not only need to name and claim the good news, but also that without that good news the sermon cannot be effective in meeting its purpose of proclaiming the gospel.

This is what good news preaching offers. It is intentional in framing the sermon around good news that represents the transformative, regenerative action of God. Good news preaching speaks to the divine/human relationship in which God is doing something in us that engages our participation, so that in effect we are prepared for and even impelled into a life of discipleship in Jesus Christ. Good news preaching takes seriously the situation of the congregation to whom the sermon will be delivered, identifies and responds specifically to the need discerned from an analysis of their situation. The good news sermon is an alternative to lulling words that deny the reality of human sin and to demanding rhetoric that lays additional burdens on the already mission-minded and often overwhelmed Christian. Good news preaching offers the covenantal grace of God that meets and responds to the reality of both human sin and human need.

In the chapters that constitute the substance of this text, I will detail how to develop and preach sermons that are intentional in offering good news. Chapter 1 lays claim to the essential nature of the sermon as good news and the importance of understanding the context and the substance of the good news from God as the beginning point of sermon development. Chapter 2 deals with the foundational nature of scripture as the source of both the sermon and the good news and interpretive models to bring the good news of the text to light. Chapter 3 focuses on the theological nature of the sermon and the necessity of appropriate theological understanding in the ongoing conversations between God, the preacher, and the people. It names the divine/human relationship that is intrinsic to an understanding of how the substance of good news operates in the lives of the people. Chapter 4 looks at the contextualization of the sermon for preaching through the juxtaposition of text and context. Chapter 5 offers practical models for developing sermons of different styles in an attempt to help preachers identify and select sermonic styles that are suited to both the scripture text that is the foundation of the sermon, and the delivery of good news for the particular context. Chapter 6 moves the sermon from the study to the pulpit and focuses on the preacher's role in giving testimony through an engaging delivery of the sermon and the effective presentation of good news. A brief concluding word is followed by four good news sermons of varying styles.

There are many persons who walked with me through the journey that brought the original text to fruition. Since its publication, some of these persons have joined the great cloud of witnesses. Despite this, I continue to thank each of them for what they poured into me and for the support that their presence gave me and pray God's blessings on their lives. Additionally, there are those who have continued to offer their support for me personally, for my work as a teacher of preaching and my writing. Specifically for the work that has led to this edition of *Good News Preaching*, I must thank my colleague at Garrett-Evangelical Theological Seminary, formerly my student, Dr. Andrew Wymer, who suggested that I approach the publisher regarding the production of a second edition of the text. And I must express my grateful appreciation to Dr. Ronald Allen, who agreed to provide a new foreword for the book and other homiletics colleagues such as Debra Mumford and David Stark, who continue to use the textbook in their classes.

Thanks also to these special persons who help to keep me grounded. They are truly God's gift to my life: My dearest friend, Denise Pickett; my niece, Charmaine Telemaque; my prayer partner, Iris Green; my teaching assistant, Seyeom Kim; friends, Indra Dorman, Jacqueline Ford, Val Hopkins, Dorrett Johnson-Agu, Janet Telemaque, and Cynella Simon; my home helpers, Marcel and Sean Johnson; my Trini friends, Ken and Cheryl Williams; Table Sisters: Cheryl Anderson, Danita Anderson, Diane Bogues, Darneather Murph-Heath, and Andrea Wright; Gen's Gems: Telly Lynette Gadson, Darlene Dellinger, Angela Hampton, Sarah Johnson, Sheron Thompson-Deas, Gwendolyn White, and Melissa Williams. Finally, thanks to my sisters Pearl and Akua Benjamin, my nephew Keithley Benjamin, and all those who offer companionship for the journey of life. There are many other persons, unnamed but greatly appreciated, who support me and my work in many ways. For all of them I give thanks and praise to God.

Finally, and above all, thank you, Holy Spirit, for your empowering wisdom.

My prayer for this text continues to be that some preacher, new or experienced, may find in its thesis and its contents a new vision for his or her task as preacher of the Word of God and may join in witness to the omnipresent grace of God through sermons that offer genuine good news to the people of God.

one

The Sermon *Is* Good News

It was the third Sunday of Advent, and the title of the sermon printed in the worship bulletin was "The Meaning of Christmas." Although I knew that there were Advent messages worthy of preaching based on the lectionary scripture texts, I was not troubled by the preacher's focus on Christmas, and I looked forward to hearing this important gospel message revealed once again. What I heard for the fifteen minutes that this preacher spoke was a history lesson on the origin of the celebration of Christmas Day—in essence, how December 25 became a Christian holiday. I was in turn stunned, disconcerted, bewildered, and finally angry. I tuned out the service as my brain went into overdrive imagining the many ways that this preacher could have helped the congregation focus on the real meaning of Christmas. Perhaps second only to his resurrection, I believe the birth of Jesus the Christ offers the most obvious good news of Christianity: how could any preacher fail to present the truly good news of Christmas, God's intentional entry into human reality, to the congregation? Observing the many blank faces in the sanctuary, I wondered what this preacher had been taught about and understood as the purpose of preaching.

Preaching is above all the proclamation of the gospel: the good news of Jesus Christ as Savior of the world. What I mean by good news being essential to the sermon is the subject of this chapter. I discuss the source of the good news, the importance of understanding the context of the congregation and its need for good news, the necessity of presenting explicitly relevant good news, and the work of the Holy Spirit in making the good news of the sermon effective in our lives. I also look at the nature of the sermon as good news in the context of worship.

A DEFINITION OF THE SERMON AS GOOD NEWS

"What is preaching?" This question is the beginning point of any class I teach or any workshop I lead on the subject of preaching. The answers in all cases are almost as many and as varied as the number of people in attendance. From my own reflection and from the many responses to that essential question, I have developed a short list of definitions that speak to the critical nature of preaching as good news. Preaching is:

- The proclamation of the gospel to the people of God in a particular time and place.
- Interpretation of the gospel to bring alive its relevance to the congregation for the shaping of their individual and communal lives.
- Helping people experience the assurance of grace that is the gospel of Jesus Christ.
- Offering the gathered community an opportunity to celebrate and claim the love of God in Jesus Christ.
- Providing guidance for interpreting and responding ethically to personal and social issues of life through the gospel.

This is by no means an exhaustive list, nor does it fully represent the various definitions offered in response to my question or those I have read over the years. What these definitions have in common is that they name as an ingredient in the sermonic construction the gospel or good news of God's grace.

Other definitions offered by my students were not so explicit but alluded to the expectation that the preacher would say something that would help people to become good or better disciples of Jesus Christ. Some respondents believed that it was the task and responsibility of the preacher to remind the hearers of their sinfulness and to call them to live according to the example of Christ. When pressed to suggest how such hearers could be helped, the respondents could seldom provide a useful solution.

That gap always helped to move the discussion to a second question: the purpose of preaching. Respondents generally agreed that preaching was about delivering the Word of God, and the preacher was identified as prophet, the mouthpiece of God who had the responsibility of delivering a message from God. In the course of ensuing conversations, respondents admitted that often the definition and the reality of preaching (as proclamation of good news) were at odds with one another. They reluctantly admitted that often more time is spent on assuring hearers of the divine inspiration of the preacher's message than on emphasizing its good news. Too often, the attention focused on ensuring that the sermon offered as many biblical sources as possible to support the preacher's position on sin and/or grace. At other times, ensuring that the style or structure of the sermon meets the expectations of the congregation took pride of place rather than the presentation of the transformative action of the divine in the face of human situations.

Expanding on the notion that the sermon has a divine origin, some students felt that while the message would vary depending on the circumstance, it should respond to the needs of the people, whatever the preacher considered them to be. And since the preacher had received the message from God, its God-directed contents did not have to be explicitly good news. That God would choose to interact with people in part through the preacher's message was good news in itself. In fact, in response to a third question on the nature of the sermon, the general response was that the sermon was a message from God. Seldom did students offer the idea that the words of the sermon were required to be recognizable as good news. Even those who named the gospel in their definition of preaching and who expressed their understanding of the good news as human redemption through Christ most often did not connect it directly with the everyday issues of life or with the need to make that good news explicit in every sermon. There was common acceptance that God's grace, active and present in human life, was good, but most expected that this was generally understood by congregations and did not need to be stated explicitly each time one preached. The purpose of the sermon, they believed, was essentially to call hearers to recognize their sin and encourage or command them to follow the teachings of Christ in order to ensure their salvation. As such, the criterion of good news was achieved by the very existence of the sermon, a message from God, which was evidence of God's presence in and interaction with the community.

I agree with students and other preachers that the sermon must be a word from God. However, as a message from God, each sermon provides the opportunity to make explicit the good news of God's redemptive, sanctifying, transformative grace that continues to be an active force in human endeavors and specifically for living as Christians. To fit its definition as good news, the sermon must make relevant to the present congregation this interaction between God and human beings in the here and now. In doing so, the message of the sermon establishes its authenticity as the Word of God, essential to hearers for living as the people of God. As Marjorie Suchocki states it, "our very lives depend upon our being hearers of God's Word."[1] As human beings and Christians, we are always in the process of becoming like Christ, such that, in the language of the Wesleyan tradition, the hope for our eternal salvation is that we are going on to perfection,[2] and the reality is that we cannot attain that state of being without the grace of God. More than that, although our hope is eternity with Christ in a state of perfection, our life in the present requires us to face trials and issues that are challenging and often unexpected. The sermon must respond to those needs in ways that offer the assurance of divine activity on our behalf. The sermon can be an effective medium for presenting the good news of God's sustaining grace that is at all times active in human endeavors, and the preacher is charged with recognizing and taking advantage of this opportunity in every moment of preaching.

For a long time, I resisted using the terms "the good news sermon" or "good news preaching" because I believed that every sermon is about proclaiming good news. My language changed as I became convinced that one ought intentionally to develop and name the good news of each sermon. Since the purpose of the sermon is to enable hearers to experience the proclamation of good news, each sermon must presumably offer good news. In scripture, prophetic messages of God's anger toward God's chosen people are always mediated by words of hope and grace. Again and again, the prophets are charged by God with offering a mitigating word to people who incurred the wrath of God because of their failure to keep the covenant. The Christian preacher likewise is charged with offering the same word of God that speaks of God's willingness to offer grace, act intentionally to bring about the transformation necessary for faithful Christian living, and enable us as human beings to deal with the vagaries of life. Recognition of this legacy is the beginning point for developing a sermon as good news.

The content of the sermon is good news when it offers evidence of the active presence and grace of God in scripture, in the life of the church, and in individual lives. But it is not simply restating history that makes this true. The sermon is good news only when its voice moves beyond echoes of the past; when the word of scripture is instructive and enlivening; when the message of God's love is recognized as timeless and delivered as active and available; and when the transformative grace of God is offered freely to all in the present as text meets context in the lives of the hearers. Although the concept of news implies and most often refers to the reporting of past events, the good news sermon as God's message is not simply anchored in past events. It is descriptive and representative of present reality and the future promise of divine-human interaction that is based on the substance of God's eternal, covenantal love for humanity revealed in scripture. Thus, the presence of explicit good news is an important element in every sermon and in every act of preaching as it enlivens, awakens, and energizes preacher and people for joyful living even in a troubled world.

THE IMPORTANCE OF NAMING GOOD NEWS IN THE SERMON

The purpose of preaching is to bring the Word of God to the congregation and specifically to offer the good news of God's love for and continued relationship with humanity. The sermon as the medium by which the preacher presents the divine word must be a proclamation of this good news. Hearing a definition of preaching as good news for the first time in a seminary preaching class jolted me, and the impact of the words sped through my system as forcefully as shock waves emanating from a disturbance in the cosmos. For a few moments, I withdrew mentally from the class. My memory of the sermons over the years that failed totally to meet this definition is what jolted me. I remembered the fire and brimstone sermons from visiting evangelists during my childhood years; the sermons that exhorted the hearers to admit their evil ways and give up such soul-destroying actions as dancing and drinking and to come forward in confession and repentance of their sin; the messages that encouraged listeners to give of their money, time, and talents; even the sermons that urged acceptance of Jesus Christ through baptism. And as my memory playback continued, only once in a while did any of these remembered sermons seem like good news in any way.

The grace of God that the professor claimed was the substance of the gospel message was either unrecognizable or absent from the sermons that flooded my mind. I was led to wonder about the interpretation of the preaching task and the content of the sermon that seemed to be the norm for Christian preachers. In fact, I questioned whether it was the seminary professor that was in error given the widespread lack of good news in sermons preached over the centuries of Christianity. Some of the same questions that emerged that day also floated through my mind on the Advent Sunday noted previously, and fortunately on both occasions I was able eventually to locate several sermons that fit the criteria of proclaiming good news. I found that among the great number of sermons that had formed me, there were those that stood out because of the affirming word they offered. And as I delved into those memories, their theme of God's free offering of redeeming love seemed to grow in importance and helped to solidify my conviction that every sermon needed to speak of the reality of God's grace that alone enables us to live faithfully as Christians. In those good news sermons of pleasant memory, the preacher had clearly presented the grace of God as active in the lives of every individual present, in their personal situations, and in the world at large, enabling those who claimed it to live fully as children of God.

We need good news in sermons not only because of our sinfulness, but also because of the challenges of life, some of which are too often overwhelming. Sin causes brokenness to both individuals and communities and is experienced not only through the physical pain and suffering of sickness and disease, but also through moral and spiritual infirmities such as injustice and oppression. Systemic ills of society perpetuate untenable situations of poverty and hunger, unemployment and homelessness, addiction and disease, and more generally the abuse and oppression of individuals and groups. The problems of violence and the evils of injustice are widespread and serve as stark reminders of the active presence of sin in the world. Beyond or perhaps because of the reality of human sinfulness, human beings find themselves confronted by challenges beyond their control. Too often we find ourselves confronted by issues that are not of our own making, but that directly impact us in myriad ways and that require the active involvement of the divine. The preacher has the responsibility to name these ills since there can be no true repentance, no ability to overcome the situation until one admits to the reality and the impact of individual and corporate sin in the world. As prophet, the preacher of the Word of God must call people to acknowledge their sinfulness, since confrontation with sin is the starting point of the way of salvation and is meant to lead the people to the act of repentance. Beyond repentance, the ability to cope with and overcome the issues and challenges that confront us requires the assurance of divine grace. From the earliest stage and throughout the process of developing the sermon, the preacher has good news to share, good news that arises from the covenantal relationship between God and human beings and that offers the assurance of God's ongoing and unending care. The preacher's task is to offer it to the listening congregation.

John Wesley named the initial act of divine love as preventing (or prevenient) grace,[3] because it prevents people from giving in to their basest human desires. Yet, we need more. Thus, in the face of sinful actions, the preacher calls hearers to seek the forgiving grace of God, for it is this forgiving grace that enables them to live according to the example of Christ and achieve holiness of heart and life. Similarly, in the face of challenges, whether of their own or because of the action of others, the preacher must offer the good news of God's transforming love in action for the lives of the people. With respect to sin, the authenticity of the sermon lies first in its ability to juxtapose divine love with human sin, and then to engage the hearts of the hearers to believe in and depend upon that love as having power against the temptations and ungodly desires that confront their hearts and minds. When it relates to specific situations or actions that confronts and impacts the people, the sermon is authentic in offering good news when it presents the grace of God in terms of its present activity in the lives of the people that transforms their situation in positive ways. Divine grace as the enabling power of Christian living is the unfailing good news that each sermon can present. Members of the congregation, confronted by life challenges, can meet or overcome them only through the grace of God. The preacher brings a message of God's unending, unfailing, expansive love that is available to all, including the preacher. But the preacher must first be convinced that divine grace applies to his or her own life in order to be able to present it as efficacious in the individual life of each congregant, the communal life of the congregation, and the world. This is the unfailing and eternal good news that is the crux of the sermon.

In order to end with good news, the preacher begins with this focus. The first step in the process requires the preacher to interrogate the situation of the congregation in order to determine the need for which the sermon is the response. Although the preacher may be charged with engaging specific texts as in Lectionary preaching, before turning to the text, the preacher evaluates the state of the congregation to identify a goal for the sermon and the means by which that goal may be realized. Once that is determined, the preacher identifies the action of God that is not only historical witness but that speaks of present action and expectant hope. A later chapter looks at methods for identifying good news in the biblical text, whether it is clearly visible in the text or not. Good news represents specific, recognizable, and transformative actions that can be attributed to God's relationship with human beings.

In order to signify that they have met the requirement of offering good news to the hearers, many students and preachers include statements in their sermon manuscripts that begin, "The good news of this sermon is." While identifying the good news of the sermon is a useful exercise for the preacher to test the contents of that sermon, there is no need to make this statement a part of the actual sermon. However, to facilitate the work of ensuring that the sermon contains good news, Allen suggests a simple formulaic exercise for preachers "to help them be sure that they are communicating good news from God in the congregation: summarize the main drift of the sermon in a single indicative sentence."[4] Such a declaration may indeed be helpful to both preacher and people, but the true necessity is to ensure that the good news is presented clearly and unambiguously such that it cannot be missed by the hearers of the sermon.

In the process of developing the good news sermon, I used a variation of Allen's model in conjunction with the biblical text in order to formulate the good news based on the needs of the people in concert with the contents of the text. The result was a sentence in which the:

- subject is God (Christ/Holy Spirit)
- the verb is the transformative action of God in human life
- the object is "us"—the human result of divine/human interaction.

The sentence thus formulated serves as a directive for creating the sermon and is used later to test that the sermon has fulfilled its purpose by meeting the stated directive. Once the Good News Statement has been created, the process of creating a good news sermon continues by connecting the good news of the text with the situation of the preaching context. Hearers will recognize it if the preacher has made the sermon's good news relevant to their situation. Although a definitive statement by the preacher may help to make it visible, if it does not emanate from scripture, if its content lacks substance, or if in the construction of the sermon the preacher has not made clear how it can transform and empower the hearers in their Christian living, no amount of emphasis will make it ring true. However, before the preacher can begin the exercise of identifying the good news in the text and framing it for the congregation, the preacher is called to determine the specific need of the congregation to which the good news should apply. The result of that exercise is the creation of a Sermon Purpose Statement.

The development of a Sermon Purpose Statement is an exercise that became an element in the development the Good News Statement after *Good News Preaching* was published. However, it is an integral part of the process of creating a good news sermon, because it enables the preacher to ensure that the contents of the sermon, and especially the good news, are relevant to the congregation within which the sermon is preached. In fact, the Sermon Purpose Statement guides the preacher in the task of ensuring that the contents of the sermon and the good news are relevant to the present situation, the feelings, and the realized or unrealized need of the congregation. By engaging the realities of the congregation on multiple levels, the preacher is able to define clearly the factors that determine the pastoral need of the ministry context and ensure that they are appropriately addressed through the sermon. Every sermon, regardless of the ministry context, is or should be developed and preached for a unique and specific purpose. This is in concert with the statement that preaching proclaims good news to a particular people in a particular time and place.

Developing the Sermon Purpose Statement brings clarity to factors in a particular preaching event that are essential for delivering relevant good news to the congregation. The three-part statement is intended to reflect the dynamics of each preaching situation. It begins with an introductory clause that describes the concern, issue, or need that is the reason for the creation of the sermon at this particular place and time. The second part of the statement suggests what the preacher wants the hearers to experience during the delivery of the sermon, which is generally more than a simple hearing of the sermon. It identifies what is expected to happen through the sermon, and particularly the impact that it is expected to have on the hearers, in light of the particular concern, issue, or need that it speaks to. However, it resists naming what would be a long-term effect on the congregation. The third and final part of the statement describes how or by what rhetorical means the hearers of the sermon will be led into the hoped-for experience. Within the statement there are key phrases that identify each of the three parts of the sermon as follows:

1. The Situation: begins with the phrase "in view of" to specify the current feelings within the congregation. For instance: *In view of* the congregation's feeling of insecurity and fear because of the violence in their community.
2. The Goal: suggests what the preacher wants the hearers *to experience*. For instance: I want the people *to experience* the assurance of God's presence and protection.

3. The Means: identifies the sermon strategy and/or the material that will be used to facilitate the hoped-for outcome. For instance: *by means of* a biblical sermon containing stories of God's care and protection in scripture and in the present.

   An example of a full Sermon Purpose Statement is as follows: *In view of* the congregation's feeling of insecurity and fear because of the violence in their community, I want the people *to experience* the assurance of God's presence and protection, *by means of* a biblical sermon containing stories of God's care and protection in scripture and in the present.

The Sermon Purpose Statement may specify the type of sermon and the biblical text on which it is based. This statement is a feeder for identifying the good news that relates to the particular congregation to whom the sermon will be preached. To facilitate the work of identifying and shaping good news from the text for the sermon, I offer a simple three-step exercise. For ease of reference, I call it the "what," "so what," and "so that" of the good news.

EXERCISE 1: WHAT IS THE GOOD NEWS OF THE TEXT?

The good news of the sermon is a definitive word of divine grace that is retrieved from the text being preached and reframed to fit the context and the purpose for which it is proclaimed. The preacher searches the substance of the text in order to unearth the specific offering of good news for the context within which it will be preached. The Good News Statement is thus representative of both the biblical text and the congregational context. Using the Sermon Purpose Statement developed above, the following provides two examples of Good News Statements that are taken from the scripture passages noted and that offer a substantive representation of divine grace in action.

> Sermon Purpose Statement
> *In view of* the congregation's feeling of insecurity and fear because of the violence in their community, I want the people *to experience* the assurance of God's presence and protection, *by means of a*

biblical sermon containing stories of God's care and protection in scripture and in the present.

Scripture Text: Matthew 9:35–38
35 Then Jesus went about all the cities and villages, teaching in their synagogues, and proclaiming the good news of the kingdom, and curing every disease and every sickness. 36 When he saw the crowds, he had compassion for them, because they were harassed and helpless, like sheep without a shepherd. 37 Then he said to his disciples, "The harvest is plentiful, but the laborers are few; 38 therefore ask the Lord of the harvest to send out laborers into his harvest."

- Good News Statement: *Christ restores us to wholeness of life.*
- Scriptural source: Matthew 9:35–36—Jesus went about all the cities and villages . . . curing every disease and every sickness.

The good news comes from Jesus' compassionate response to the needs of the people, healing them in body, mind, and spirit and so offering them wholeness of heart and life. Through Jesus' response to the needs of the people, their situations are transformed and they are empowered to live in new ways. The good news selected from this text is readily apparent since the idea of God's compassion is recognizable as good news. It is appropriate to the context described in the Sermon Purpose Statement, because it represents people who are in a similar state as those in the biblical text, although the cause of their situation is different. Because of the fear and insecurity of the congregation, their spirits are less than they should be. Therefore, they need restoration to be whole. However, in many instances there are multiple representations of good news contained in a single text—for example, the request for additional laborers may be presented as good news—and the preacher's choice of one will depend on the context in which the sermon is to be preached.

In some cases, as shown in the following example, the good news is not as overt, but still discernible in the text.

Jeremiah 29:1, 4–7
These are the words of the letter that the prophet Jeremiah sent from Jerusalem to the remaining elders among the exiles, and to the priests, the prophets, and all the people, whom Nebuchadnezzar had taken into exile from Jerusalem to Babylon. Thus says the LORD of hosts, the God of Israel, to all the exiles whom I have sent into exile from Jerusalem to Babylon: Build houses and live in them; plant gardens and eat what they produce. Take wives and have sons and daughters; take wives for your sons, and give your daughters in marriage, that they may bear sons and daughters; multiply there, and do not decrease. But seek the welfare of the city where I have sent you into exile, and pray to the LORD on its behalf, for in its welfare you will find your welfare.

- Good News Statement: *God directs us in our times of uncertainty.*

The message from God in the mouth of the prophet Jeremiah speaks of God's continued active concern for and involvement in the lives of the people, who are living in a state of exile. Through the prophet, God directs the exiled people in the way that they should continue to live as people of the covenant. Through the good news of the covenantal love of God in action, the sermon offers the listening congregation a word of hope in the midst of their real-life situation of fear and uncertainty that in a sense make them exiles from the security that they desire in their lives.

In both cases, the scripture as good news offers God's grace in action; the good news may be used to bridge the historical realities of the cultures of the text and those of the present. Once it is identified, asking "so what?" of the good news allows the preacher to make it relevant to the context of the hearers of the sermon.

EXERCISE 2: ASK THE "SO WHAT?" QUESTION OF THE GOOD NEWS STATEMENT

Scripture provides evidence of God's redeeming, restorative love in historical contexts. Likewise, the church maintains records of God's presence and power in the lives of individual Christians and the redeemed community over time. Yet these historical records are not the substance of the good news of the sermon. In a later chapter we will discuss the importance of contextualization for developing and preaching effective sermons; for now, it is enough to say that the good news one delivers needs to be directly related to the needs of the hearers. Asking a "so what?" question of the good news extracted from the text is one way of determining the appropriateness of the good news.

Why is this so? Because it helps to identify connections between the good news of the text and its impact on both the need identified in the Sermon Purpose Statement and in developing the hearers as Christian disciples. The Good News Statement is directed to the hearers and speaks of God's action in enabling them to live fully as Christians despite their present circumstances. The "so what?" question is intrinsic to the process of preaching and helps the preacher give focus to the purpose and content of each sermon. Unless the sermon answers this question specifically, it will not connect directly with the congregation. Hearers of the sermon want to apply its message of good news to their individual lives.

The "so what?" question as the second step speaks to the specific needs of the particular hearers, the application of God's grace to those needs, and the hoped-for response of the hearers to the message of the sermon. The answer to the "so what?" question provides direction for the message of discipleship that will result from the good news of the sermon. It directs the creation of a Discipleship Message Statement that connects the good news of the sermon with the life of the hearers. Answering the "so what?" question in light of the context of the people's lives, as described in the Sermon Purpose Statement, enables the preacher to ensure that not only the good news, but also the discipleship action to be taken in response to the good news allows the hearers to live into the transformative action of God's grace that the sermon presents. Applying the "so what?" test to the Good News Statements developed in the first exercise may yield the following results:

- Scripture text: Matthew 9:35–38
- Good News Statement: *Christ restores us to wholeness of life.*
- Response to the "so what?" question: *So that we can live full and abundant lives.*

The reason that the congregation needs to receive the good news of the restorative grace of God in Jesus Christ is that the situation in the community is generating fear and a sense of insecurity, which is curtailing their lives. In the text, Jesus has been healing the brokenness caused by the sickness and disease that was believed to be the result of sin. For the present congregation, Jesus Christ, God's gift of grace to all humanity, restores a sense of security despite the conditions that surround them in the community. Even though the situation between the biblical text and the present context is very different, both resulted in a sense of lack that reduced the fullness of life that should be experienced and enjoyed by every person. The restoration in each case brings wholeness and enables abundant living.

- Scripture text: Jeremiah 29:1, 4–7
- Good News Statement: *God directs us in our times of fear and uncertainty.*

Response to the "so what?" question: So that we can experience the assurance that God's presence gives.

The Sermon Purpose Statement described a situation that prohibited the people from experiencing wholeness in life because of their fear and uncertainty. The good news of God's guidance for the exiled Israelites delivers a beacon of hope and can be the catalyst for offering good news for dealing with their situation. As the congregation receives the good news of divine presence in the situation of the text, they can also receive reassurance for their times of fear and uncertainty in the present or for the future.

The third and final step of this exercise is to develop a Discipleship Message Statement. This statement names the action that emanates from the good news and directs or supports the hearers in their action as Christian disciples. Encouraging such action is ultimately the goal of every sermon. It frames the purpose of the good news as a call to action, as an imperative statement that offers a directive for Christian discipleship. It directs and guides the hearers in applying the good news of the text, and ultimately of the sermon, through practical implementation in their lives.

EXERCISE 3: CREATE A DISCIPLESHIP MESSAGE STATEMENT THAT PROVIDES DIRECTION FOR THE ACTION OF DISCIPLESHIP.

The Discipleship Message Statement is important for concluding the good news sermon because it moves the good news forward into the life of the hearers by providing a call to action that affects or influences the hearers' lives as disciples of Jesus Christ. Good news preaching not only offers transformative good news to hearers, but also calls, invites, instructs, directs, or even urges hearers to move forward in living as Christian disciples through the application of the good news in their lives. The Sermon Purpose Statement offers a goal toward which the preacher moves in the construction of the sermon, and the Discipleship Message Statement offers a directive for the lives of the hearers going forward beyond the hearing of the sermon. The Discipleship Message Statement calls for specific activity on the part of the hearers that is directed by the good news garnered from the text. It is purposeful and missional, and it gives evidence of the enabling grace of God in the divine/human relationship.

There is no specific formula for creating a Discipleship Message Statement but, unlike the Good News Statement, the subject, whether named or implied, is human beings, and the verb is an imperative that invites action on the part of the hearers of the good news. In developing the Discipleship Message Statement, students often connect the Good News Statement with the conjunctive phrase "so that" in order to arrive at a statement that can direct the hearers to act in particular ways. The preacher moves beyond the "so what?" in order to name the particular action that the hearers must engage that is in accord with their Christian discipleship. The following are suggested message statements created from the Good News Statements and the responses to the "so what?" question in the two previous exercises:

- Scripture text: Matthew 9:35–38
- Good News Statement: *Christ restores us to wholeness of life.*
- Response to the "so what?" question: So that we can live full and abundant lives.
- Discipleship Message Statement: *Live confidently through the assurance of Christ's presence in your life.*

- Sermon Purpose Statement: In view of *the congregation's feeling of insecurity and fear because of the violence in their community, I want the people* to experience *the assurance of God's presence and protection*, by means of *a biblical sermon containing stories of God's care and protection in scripture and in the present.*

The purpose of the sermon is to reassure listeners that just as Christ responded with compassion to the needs of the biblical crowds, Christ will do the same for today's hearers as they are beset by fear and uncertainty because of their life situation. The sermon can encourage the hearers to have faith that they will experience wholeness of heart and life through Jesus Christ instead of fear and uncertainty, which will in turn allow them to live an abundant life. The preacher makes clear in the sermon how one accepts and lives fully and abundantly beyond fear through the presence of Christ.

- Scripture text: Jeremiah 29:1, 4–7
- Good News Statement: *God directs us in our times of fear and uncertainty.*
- Response to the "so what?" question: So that we can at all times trust God for guidance regardless of the situation.
- Discipleship Message Statement: *Trust God to guide and support you in every situation.*
- Purpose of the sermon: To connect with the feelings of fear and uncertainty that hearers are suffering and instill hope and courage in the congregation so that even when they feel lost (as though exiled), they will trust that God continues to provide support and direction for their lives whatever the circumstances.

The exercise of naming what good news from the text will direct the sermon, determining its applicability to the context by means of the "so what?" question, and naming a specific charge so that the hearers will live into the sermonic good news, while essential to good news preaching, is not an exact science. It is simply an exercise that helps to ensure that the sermon is intentional in offering good news. Once the sermon is written, the preacher is encouraged to test its contents against this material and modify or change completely whatever is necessary to ensure that the sermon offers appropriate good news and a discipleship message that connects with the life of the hearers.

THE SOURCE OF THE GOOD NEWS

The source of the good news is always God. The good news derives not just from a single passage in the Bible but from the entire message of scripture and from the deepest theological beliefs of the church concerning God, Jesus Christ, and the Holy Spirit. Evidence of the grace of God is present in the words of scripture, and the preacher retrieves it and at times must struggle to decipher it in the midst of language that is often perverted and strange. But it is not the text itself, no matter how inspiring, that contains the good news. It is God working through the text to untangle the good news from the often convoluted streams of text and historical contexts; God working through the preacher to disengage beliefs and biases and to destroy filters that misappropriate or misinterpret the words of scripture; and God working through the people in the present and active contexts of their individual and corporate lives to bring to their attention the revelation and assurance of divine grace. It is God speaking that brings to life the Word of God that challenges, moves, or impels the hearers to connect with the good news in transforming ways. God in scripture and in life as lived in the present still speaks, and God is the source of the message of good news that must be delivered to the people. God, the originator, determines the content of the message that the preacher delivers.

The challenge for preachers is to hear correctly the message of God for the people. The preacher stands in the midst of the people and must also stand sufficiently apart from them in order to hear the Word of God that arises from the text that is being preached and that at the same time connects with the context in which it will be preached. In this way, past and present connect through a divine word that transcends time and space, and the preacher gives voice to it in a way that can engage minds and hearts to hear the Word of God in all its fullness. God's word moves through history and into the present and is contextualized in the sermon to address the gathered community. Just as it does not emanate simply from the text, neither does the good news emanate simply from the community. The good news message of the sermon is not simply what the community wants to hear, but what it needs to hear to be delivered from its present situation, and even from the sin that besets human life.

Although I am advocating the idea of good news as critical to preaching, experience over time has shown that the beginning point in the development of the sermon and the delivery of relevant good news must be the creation of a Sermon Purpose Statement. I recommend strongly that preachers start by listening intently to the congregation to understand their situation and the feelings they are experiencing. That understanding becomes directive for the good news that needs to be delivered to the congregation. Developing a message of good news and creating a Good News Statement demands intentionally drawing upon this understanding. Since God is the source of the message, it behooves the preacher to listen to what God is saying to both preacher and people. Such active listening to God is part of good sermon preparation and facilitates the creation of a sermon that offers a message that impacts and even transforms the hearers as Christian disciples. The Good News Statement thus names the transformative action of divine love, whereas the Discipleship Message statement names the action that is the hoped-for response of the hearers to the divine love in action.

There is a singular point to every sermon, in whatever shape it is constructed, and that is to offer God's word of divine grace. The manner in which this word is couched is based on the art of the preacher, and the preacher's presentation either offers encouragement or causes the hearer to turn away from the word of truth. How the preacher understands the congregation's needs directly affects how the preacher interprets the biblical text. When the two meld, the preacher's words come to life as the divine word. In this way the preacher is not impelled to seek outside voices for some "good news" and is not tempted or driven to assume the dual role of source and authority of good news to the detriment of the sermon.

Edmund A. Steimle, responding to Karl Barth's statement that "[p]reaching is the Word of God which he himself has spoken," asks, "How is a preacher to determine the difference between his words and the Word of God?"[5] To do so, the preacher must be engaged in active, ongoing communication with God in order to become familiar with God's voice, and thus be able to differentiate between words and Word. Yet the preacher is not the only one with whom God is communicating. For the good news to fit the people to whom it is proclaimed, the preacher must also be in communication with the people so that the words of the sermon can offer them an appropriate message of God's grace.

Often, preachers are moved, inspired, and sometimes even compelled to call the people of God to an accounting of their sinful state as the biblical prophets did in their time. However, as prophets and like the biblical prophets, preachers today must also speak a word of hope, and above all, of divine love. Unless the sermon contains this, it cannot rightly be called the Word of God. At the same time, it is insufficient and unworthy of their prophetic role for preachers to speak only of God's grace without calling the people to an understanding of the sin that is mitigated by that grace, and the need for repentance, which is the evidence of their understanding and acceptance of God's grace. In light of the reality of human sin, God's unfailing grace manifest in the sermon makes the sermon a fit offering for its recipients.

Steimle speaks directly to this point when he questions "whether there are many congregations left today who listen dutifully and reverently to their minister's sermon as the Word of God which he himself has spoken."[6] Indeed, how can they and why should they if that purported Word of God contains no recognizable good news? And yet, if the sermon is explicit in proclaiming God and specifically how the love of God is actively working to bring about transformation in the life of the gathered community for the sake of the world, then they will hear the good news that they need and should expect from a sermon.

CENTERING THE SERMON IN GOOD NEWS

Making a general statement about God, such as "God loves" or "God wishes," is insufficient for offering transformative good news. Yes, God does love, and God does wish. However, unless the preacher specifies the form taken by the divine/human interaction, it is unlikely to impact hearers as they move forward in their lives as redeemed Christians. In the same way, creating a Good News Statement that simply defines a divine characteristic, such as "God is love," is just as unhelpful in providing transformative good news. The action verbs suggested for use in a Good News Statement must speak clearly not only of God's continual work in the redemption of humanity but also of the transformation or empowerment it provides to those who have made the commitment to live into their identity as the re- deemed children of God. The good news of God's saving action becomes more than a source of encouragement to the hearers, more than an invitation to continue on the path of Christian perfection. It offers the hearers confirmation of the enabling force of God's active presence and grace that facilitate their continued life in Christ and their continuing transformation leading to Christian perfection.

In presenting "A Brief Theology of Preaching," David Buttrick notes that "in our preaching Christ continues to speak to the church and through the church to the world. Preaching is the preaching of Jesus Christ because it opens to us salvific new life and discloses the reality of God-toward-us."[7] With respect to good news preaching, what the preacher discloses is the reality of how God actively participates in human endeavors, which enables humanity to be both participants in and exponents of God's grace. The sermon as purveyor of the message cannot shirk its responsibility of presenting divine grace in recognizable form. The preacher must make evident the offer of new life in a way that entices the engagement of hearers.

Earlier, I named the issue of the preacher engaging in communication with God as important and even critical to the preacher's ability to hear the divine word. Likewise, it is necessary that the preacher have a defined theology of preaching. The basis of all interpretation of the biblical text must be theological, for it is through the lens of a preacher's theology that they understand God. Only by wrestling with the issues of divine presence is there the possibility or the hope that the words of scripture can become the Word of God for the people of God. In order to engage the text in a way that reveals the grace of God toward humanity, the preacher must be in harmony with the message of God that emanates from the biblical text.

The listening ear hears and interprets as the mind conceives. If the preacher does not understand God as grace, then the sermon is in jeopardy of being only useful pastoral advice that is sorely lacking the incarnational spark necessary to make of ordinary persons witnesses and messengers of Christ. The Spirit of God must breathe life into both the preacher and the words of the sermon in order for them to become saturated with and transformed by God's grace. In this way, the good news that began as a simple statement takes shape as the nucleus of the message and permeates all aspects of the sermon—content, creation, and delivery. As Fred Craddock explains, "If preaching is in any way a continuation into the present of God's revelation, then what we are doing and how we are doing it should be harmonious with our understanding of the mode of revelation. In other words, from the transaction we call revelation we understand and implement the transaction we call preaching."[8] Preaching good news is the preacher's participation in the ongoing drama of human life, which is rich and free through living fully in the grace of God.

THE HOLY SPIRIT AS AGENT OF GOOD NEWS

Preaching is impossible without the presence of the Holy Spirit. The sermon cannot be effective unless it is truly the Word of God, and that is not possible without the presence of the Holy Spirit. Like the bones in Ezekiel's vision, even with flesh and sinews, the sermon has no power to move the hearers without the breath of God giving it life. An effective sermon is founded on scripture, well-constructed, theologically appropriate, sensitive to its time, place, and context, and delivered with conviction. It is good news presented by the preacher and received by the hearers for the continued growth of the body of Christ. This is a daunting task, and it cannot be accomplished unless the Holy Spirit permeates the words and the preacher. In his farewell speech, Jesus promised the disciples that he would send the Holy Spirit to provide everything they needed to continue the work he had started (John 17:7–8), and the biblical witness tells of the outpouring of the promised Spirit on the day of Pentecost (Acts 2:1–21). We also learn from scripture that the grace of Christ gives the gifts necessary for the ongoing life of the church. Paul assures the Ephesians (4:7–16) that Christ has given varied gifts for building up the church for its work of ministry, and to the Corinthians he names the Holy Spirit as the source of all gifts (1 Corinthians 12:1–11). Since Jesus Christ named the Holy Spirit as the one who would give power to the disciples for their work, we too can name the Holy Spirit as the source of power necessary to proclaim the word of God.

Paul implies that preachers have a special call from God (Romans 10), and that preaching itself is a spiritual gift, given by God and empowered by the Holy Spirit. As Marjorie Suchocki puts it, "God's word comes to us as a whisper. It is not loud, like a clanging cymbal, nor is it boisterous, calling attention to itself. To the contrary, it is a quiet word, a suggestive word, an inviting word, not always easily noticed."[9] Thus, the preacher, called and gifted for the task, must listen intently for God's whispered message of hope and grace for the community. An earlier statement that bears repeating is that the preacher must be in active communication with God in order to hear the whispered message that God sends to the people via the preacher.[10] Not only must the preacher listen to the initiating whispers of God, they must maintain that communication with the divine throughout the entire process of sermon development and look to the Holy Spirit for guidance on how to deliver the sermon. The Holy Spirit facilitates the church's hearing of the good news that exists in all of scripture and makes of the preaching event a moment of worship and celebration for the people of God.

James Forbes believes that "the person who preaches the gospel makes a statement about the Holy Spirit just by entering the pulpit."[11] Like Forbes, I believe that through divine-human communication, the Holy Spirit guides the preacher in the selection of the biblical text for preaching, whether or not the lectionary is followed. Such divine guidance takes into consideration the needs of both preacher and people and directs the preacher through all the steps of preparing for preaching. Long before thoughts become words or phrases or sounds, it is the Holy Spirit that prompts preachers in the direction that the sermon needs to follow. In order to benefit from the agency of the Holy Spirit, preachers must allow sufficient time for meditation on scripture, for prayer and personal devotion, and even for silent reflection and active listening for the divine voice. Active listening through spoken prayer and silent reflection helps preachers to recognize God's voice as they prepare to speak God's Word.

So how does one recognize the voice of God? How does one become attuned to the presence of the Holy Spirit in the development and preaching of the sermon? The preacher who has been in communication with God will understand the need to test the thoughts of the mind and the inclinations of the heart in the light of God's love for all people. In other words, if the preacher's message focuses exclusively on leveling accusations of sin without offering the mitigating grace of God, it is unlikely that the message originated from the Holy Spirit. The Holy Spirit as the power of God is the promised gift of Christ to comfort, support, and sustain the people of God. It is offered because of the need for God's grace—intrinsic to all human life—and the Holy Spirit speaks the divine word into the truth of human fallibility. Likewise, if the preacher seeks to bypass the reality of sin in a misguided effort to spare the people from facing their humanness, the news offered as good is worthless. The Holy Spirit speaks into and against the reality of sin and offers a redemptive word in all circumstances. The preacher who listens for this dual focus is assured in the hearing: it is the voice of God.

Forbes reminds us that the preacher must be anointed for the task of preaching. He cites the anointing of Jesus "as a model of spiritual formation"[12] and notes the common though erroneous belief that anointing is a one-time event. The preacher needs the anointing of the Holy Spirit for every occasion of preaching and at every step in the process of developing and preaching the sermon. Jesus himself claimed the anointing of God for his own ministry (Luke 4:16–22) and the preacher needs the same in order to create and deliver each sermon. Thus, anointed by the Holy Spirit, the preacher is empowered to be God's representative and can fulfill the role of messenger of God. This anointing is not the result of critical study of the biblical text, or of superior hermeneutical or theological knowledge. It is a gift of God. Preachers who open themselves to God experience this grace more readily. With Jesus as a model, the preacher's life is open and available to God to be used for the building up of the church. Just as Jesus' anointing was not for his own sake, so too the anointing of the preacher is not for personal gain or acclamation, but for the church.

As the agent of good news, the Holy Spirit is present with the gathered community—preacher and hearers—and the event of preaching in the midst of the community may be recognized as one aspect of the broader work of the Spirit to nurture, empower, and guide the church so that it may serve Christ in its service to the world. The people as hearers play as active a part in the preaching task as the preacher, because preaching is a component of the conversations between God and the preacher, God and the people, and the preacher and the people. The relationship between God and the people is as informative for the preacher in determining the substance of the sermon as is the preacher's own conversation with God. Through the preacher's conversation with the people, the Holy Spirit speaks into being the message of good news that is appropriate to the needs of the people in that particular time and place.

THE SERMON AS GOOD NEWS IN THE CONTEXT OF WORSHIP

In the same way that the Holy Spirit calls and empowers the preacher for the task, so too the Holy Spirit gathers the people for worship, which includes the preaching and hearing of God's word. Worship is the people's response to God's self-revelation in the midst of the gathered community. To my mind, that includes preaching. As good news of God's grace, the sermon is evidence of God's self-revelation and therefore worthy of the celebratory response of the gathered community. Celebration of God's presence in all of life is intrinsic to the act of worship for which the people of God gather. The experience and rituals of worship enable the people of God to give voice in praise and acclamation to being recipients of God's grace, and the sermon is one representation of that voice.

Frank Thomas, following in the footsteps of his mentor Henry Mitchell, studied the role of celebration in African American preaching.[13] He looks back to "the early New Testament community (that) understood Jesus Christ himself to be the good news"[14] and therefore worthy of celebrating whenever the church gathered. In describing this celebratory motif of African American preaching, Thomas focuses on the good news of Jesus' salvific act as the source and reason for celebration in the sermon. However, his focus on the second Testament leaves one wondering whether good news is not also found in the first Testament. The celebration of God's grace begins with creation and continues throughout biblical history. It is present in the law and the prophets in God's covenantal love for the Hebrew people, a constant amidst their human failures that repeatedly led them to wander away from the worship of Yahweh and reject God's directives. God's presence, protection, and grace throughout scripture evoke a celebratory response from all who live within that legacy. That response is not contingent on a celebratory style of sermon, but the preacher who understands that sermons celebrate God's grace will make sure that celebration defines its message. People's celebration in response to the good news that they have received is an act of worship. It may be initiated or continued through the preached sermon, and the response of the hearers may be evidenced in changed lives that result in more faithful discipleship. Preaching is thus a celebratory act of God's people, which helps to shape and define the ongoing life of the gathered community.

Preaching is liturgical because preaching occurs only in the context of worship. Too often, regardless of the situation or context, the delivery of an unwanted message is referred to as preaching. And while it may be too late to reclaim this colloquial definition from its usage in both society and the church, the preacher has the opportunity to remind the church that it is the agent of proclamation of God's message of salvation. Proclaiming a message of good news in every sermon may begin to remove the stigma that seems to surround the activity of preaching, because it means being faithful to the eternal grace of God revealed in all of scripture and calls Christians of every age and stage of life to a celebratory response of worship and praise.

By being intentional and explicit about proclaiming good news, the sermon offers its hearers a glimpse into the mind of God, who accepts each person and offers to each unending grace. The sermon is good news when it connects and reconnects the people of God with the assurance of God's presence as the fulfillment of the divine/human covenant and, above all, when it enables the people of God through worship to acknowledge and confess the presence of God in all the vagaries of their human lives. The preacher delves into the words of scripture to unearth the word of life to share with the people in a particular time and place. The sermon is good news when God's presence with preacher and people is not only instructive but empowering.

two

Laying the Biblical Foundations for the Good News

It was the first evening of the basic preaching class and, in the process of reviewing the syllabus, I repeated a statement that was printed as one of the goals of the class: that by the completion of the term, students should understand the Bible as foundational to preaching. A challenge came from a student who had seemed to become more and more troubled as I explained the contents of the syllabus. This student considered my statement problematic and said: "I can produce a good sermon on Thoreau." Of course, I disagreed. Many years later, I continue to maintain the position that I expounded to the students in my class that evening. At the heart of my disagreement was the belief then and now that the foundation of Christian proclamation is faith in God as creator, redeemer, and sustainer of our lives. And while the presence of God in human life is both past and present, the Bible as our book of faith offers a basis for understanding the divine. As I told the student that night, his experience of Thoreau's work could provide support for his understanding of God, but it is insufficient to be the basis of proclamations about God. However, having listened to too many sermons that were short on scripture or lacking it entirely, I know that there are those who hold a similar belief that it is possible to construct a sermon based only on a source other than scripture.

That I consider scripture foundational for preaching does not dismiss or diminish the place of other materials in the sermon. Indeed, the inclusion of non-biblical material can add greater depth and clarity to our understanding of the biblical word. However, since we believe that scripture is the Word of God, and that the preacher is charged to offer the Word of God to the people, then from my perspective, it stands to reason that the sermon should begin with what has already been accepted as the inspired Word of God. I say inspired because I decry any attempt, regardless of how scholarly the argument may be, to claim that the contents of the Bible were spoken directly out of the mouth of God. As a document of human creation, even inspired, the Bible includes materials that I find challenging, especially as they have been and are used to perpetuate the evils of oppression and injustice against individuals and groups in the world. And although scholars have long debated the inerrancy of the biblical texts, this does not diminish the divine inspiration that brought the Bible into being and that is necessary to create the sermon that offers good news.

The preacher engages scripture to discern its relevance as the Word of God for particular people in a particular time and place. Having faithfully delved into the text and unearthed its meaning for preaching in the present context, the preacher becomes the vessel by which the gospel is proclaimed, and the words of the sermon become the medium through which the Word of God is delivered to the people. Homileticians and preachers in general have accepted that only through divine mystery can the words spoken by the preacher become the Word of God, and only as the Word of God can the words of the sermon be effective in transforming the minds and hearts of the hearers. As Eugene Lowry puts it, "preaching the sermon is a task; proclaiming the Word is the hoped-for goal."[1] The ability of that task to reach its goal, however, is partly dependent on the preacher's ability to search deeply into the words of scripture and impart its truth to the gathered congregation. Biblical interpretation lays a foundation on which to support the accuracy or appropriateness of the good news of the sermon. Analyzing how the good news might speak into the situation of those to whom it is being delivered is equally important and absolutely necessary.

This chapter looks at how we approach the scripture text to identify the good news and interpret it for our context. In order to appropriate the good news of the text for the context of preaching, both text and context require interpretation, or exegesis. In the exegetical process, I give as much attention to unearthing good news from scripture for the preaching context as I do to interpreting the context in which the scripture will be preached. In this way, the interpretive work of exegesis connects the content of the scripture text or texts with the people of God in the present. However, especially as the context of the lives of the hearers are in a constant state of flux, based on the constant and rapidly changing world, understanding the context in which the sermon will be delivered is critical and must be done carefully even before the interpretation of the text is begun. Also, as part of this interpretive process, I determine the style or structure of the sermon. The choice of sermon style is also dependent in part on an analysis of the context in which the sermon will be preached. This is critical when one is a guest preacher, but it is also important for the pastor/preacher who is addressing a familiar congregation. The host congregation might ask a guest preacher to address a particular theme in light of a special event in the church. That may be done through the lens of a particular scripture passage or by applying the theme more widely by using several texts. On the other hand, the pastor/preacher may follow the lectionary readings for weekly sermons but must still choose the text most suited to the congregation's need of the moment. Whatever the reason for the preacher's selection of sermon type and scripture text or texts, ensuring that the sermon offers good news that emanates from scripture and that is applicable to the hearers necessitates interpretation of both text and context.

SERMON TYPES—BIBLICAL EXPOSITORY OR TOPICAL

In concert with the interpretive work of text and context, the preacher decides on the type of sermon type for the occasion—biblical expository or topical. A biblical expository sermon breaks open a text or texts, allowing the interpretation of the texts to be applied to the context and showing its relevance for that congregation. A topical sermon brings light to a particular topic or theme (such as God's faithfulness) and reveals its applicability to the moment of preaching.

In biblical expository preaching, the purpose of the sermon is to help the congregation interpret its situation through the lens of a biblical passage. The development of the sermon centers in the exegesis, theological analysis, and hermeneutical appropriation of the biblical material. John McClure emphasizes the centrality and the authority of scripture for the biblical expository sermon. "First, preachers strive to understand the biblical text on its own terms as much as possible apart from their own personal or doctrinal agendas. [S]econd, [they strive for] clarity in communication."[2] Yet the focus on scripture cannot distract the preacher from ensuring that its intrinsic good news comes alive or showing its relevance to the present.

In topical preaching, the preacher helps the congregation interpret a topic from the perspective of the gospel. Topical sermons typically address a Christian doctrine or practice, a personal or social situation. The topical sermon also has a biblical foundation, but it does not center on the exposition of a biblical text in the same way as the biblical expository sermon. Instead, it is the people's needs that direct the preacher's attention to the topic and then engages it theologically and biblically. Because it connects directly with congregational needs many preachers use topical preaching for special occasions in the life of the congregation. Although the initial focus is different from the biblical expository sermon, topical sermons also require a foundation of a biblical text, but Ronald Allen offers this cautionary word against bringing together unrelated texts under the banner of a particular topic, warning that "in all cases the integrity of the Bible is to be honored."[3]

The biblical record of God's covenantal relationship and God's direct and indirect action in the lives of human beings offers a window through which people can see and understand God's unwavering presence and grace in human life. But while the Bible speaks clearly of God's presence, its truths are often hidden in the cobwebs of history and language and interpretation, so the preacher's task is to decipher its context and meaning. Even today, the Bible brings a relevant word and is a continuing source of revelation of God's everlasting presence in the world. The preacher's decision on sermon type depends on the preaching context and the people's needs. In fact, the reality is that all sermons are pastoral in the sense that the pastor reviews the situation of the congregation in order to decide the type and structure of the sermon that is appropriate for the particular event of preaching. For example, the preacher may give a series of biblical expository sermons to develop biblical knowledge in a congregation that resists the discipline of Bible study. Likewise, a series of topical sermons may serve to address the overall subject of discipleship, mission, or some other Christian doctrine or practice. This pastoral decision is made in concert with the Sermon Purpose Statement, where the pastor/preacher delineates the situation of the congregation, the goal of the sermon, and how the sermon will achieve the stated goal. That decision includes the style of the sermon. Once the preacher has decided, he or she selects the supporting text or texts and begins the task of interpretation. A preacher begins the exegetical process for both the biblical expository and the topical sermon by identifying the good news for the context in which the sermon will be preached and heard. In other words, how the preacher interprets the biblical text depends on the human context of the preaching moment.

BIBLICAL EXEGESIS: AN INTERPRETIVE PROCESS

Biblical exegesis is about offering a critical explanation or interpretation of a biblical text. It requires that the reader delve deeply into the scripture passage to unearth its meaning. In one of his early texts, Ronald Allen describes biblical exegesis as "concerned with recovering the historical background of the text."[4] In a later text he expands his definition of the term to be "the disciplined process of locating the possible meanings of a text in its historical, literary, and theological contexts."[5] In both cases, his definition refers to the process of peeling back the layers of history surrounding the location within which the text has been anchored in order to offer it in the present as the biblical word. Biblical exegesis thus offers a snapshot of biblical history.

What did the text mean in its original context? What situation caused the text to be written? What is the situation of which the text speaks? What is the text's literary form and how does that influence our reading and understanding of the text? A preacher asks these and many other questions as part of the historical analysis. The historical picture is revelatory—with respect to the good news of divine grace and to the way in which the people represented in the text understood the nature of God and their place in the divine plan. Such exegetical work also identifies the first hearers of the text and the place and function of the text in their lives. More important for good news preaching, biblical exegesis works to uncover the layers of history between which lie the essence of the divine/human encounter and its silent witness to God's eternal grace.

The answers to the historical questions may challenge the preacher at many levels and may lure the preacher to bypass the historical reality of the text in favor of a more palatable interpretation. However, beyond its historicity, the literary form of the text may suggest or determine how it is preached. Its literary construction, key words, and historical exigencies may have significant influence on sermonic form and content. In addition, a preacher's inability to research or review the text in its original language may obscure meaning that does not translate clearly into modern-day English. Yet somehow the past must meet the present; the preacher must be able to unpack the text and offer its good news for each occasion of preaching.

When the intent of preaching is to offer transformative good news to the hearers, we broaden the exegetical process to include more than the interpretation of the text or topic. Exegesis should also interpret the context of preaching in order to determine the nature of good news that will be appropriate and applicable to the hearers. In the same way that we investigate each text to bring to light its full meaning, so too we investigate the congregation to unearth the historical and present situations that will affect the people's ability to hear and take to heart the good news. The context of preaching requires specific interpretive attention because it is the connection between text and context that gives substance to the offering of divine grace in the sermon.

Occasionally, the preacher may address a topic for preaching during the investigation of a particular biblical text, such as the issue of faith in the process of healing, as seen in one of Jesus' healing miracles recorded in the gospels. In such cases, the selection of the text precedes the choice of preaching topically, as the style of the sermon and the exegesis of the text ensures that the emergent topic is actually contained in or relevant to the text. Still, many topical sermons are focused on a particular Christian doctrine or practice. Since the foundation of ecclesial doctrines is theological, and in most cases, biblical, the preacher should use one or more texts in the process of interpreting the topic. When the preacher begins with the topic, he or she determines the good news that is relevant for the hearers based on both theological investigation and the context of the hearers. Only when this topical analysis is done should the preacher select scriptures that engage the topic and become the basis of the good news preached.

HOMILETICAL EXEGESIS

In teaching exegesis for preaching, I use the term homiletical exegesis as a way of including both exegesis of the biblical text or the topic and the context in which the sermon will be preached. Homiletical exegesis follows a methodology similar to biblical interpretation, and indeed borrows from it. However, it begins with an awareness of the present situation of the congregation that not only sheds light on the applicability of the biblical or topical interpretation, but also gives insight as to the good news that needs to be shared with the hearers.

Homiletical exegesis for good news preaching includes contextual analysis to gain an understanding of the social, cultural, ecclesial, or other human situation of the congregation to determine the prevailing situation of the location where the sermon will be preached. It includes historical, literary, and theological methodologies of biblical interpretation, which it combines with contextual analysis in order to give the preacher an authentic platform from which to launch the sermonic message of good news to the people of God. It assumes that the preacher accepts scripture as the true record of God's presence in human endeavors and that they have a sound theology that acknowledges the covenantal grace of God as an affirming, enlivening love that is available to all people.

Prerequisite to the basic preaching class at my seminary are introductory courses in both Testaments, where students are taught appropriate methods of biblical interpretation. In addition, students must take at least one theology course that serves to anchor their understanding of God as they encounter various aspects of the divine nature in scripture. Also, because homiletical exegesis is a combination of biblical exegesis and contextual analysis, a basic pastoral care course may be beneficial for understanding the context of the congregation. However, it is the preacher's commitment to offering good news that facilitates the creation of a sermon that encourages Christian discipleship, or that calls nonbelievers to become disciples of Jesus Christ. That is the prerequisite for the overall exegetical process.

In order to accomplish genuine good news preaching through the exposition of a chosen biblical text or topic, the preacher begins at the place of anticipation, where the hope of promise is met with the reality of fulfillment. That means that the process of exegeting the text does not begin with the interrogation of the text to identify its good news, but with the anticipation or expectation that there is good news in the text or topic for preaching. I typically approach homiletical exegesis for good news sermons by addressing three sets of questions directed at:

- Analysis of the congregation—the situation of preaching and the specific shape or content of the good news it requires.
- Identification of good news—recognizable or hidden in the text or the topic.
- Interpretation of the biblical text or the topic—the historical, literary, and other critical elements that facilitate recognition of good news in the text or topic.

Systematic contextual and biblical interpretation enables the preacher to appropriately apply the substance of the text in its contextual framework, and therefore it is important to develop a discipline of exegetical work for every sermon. When the preacher neglects the interpretive work, the sermon is often rudderless and not only fails to apply to the congregation, but also drifts away from the scripture passage it is meant to expound upon. On the other hand, when the preacher focuses only on study exegesis and turns it into sermon exegesis, the sermon becomes a paper or report; it ceases to be a sermon that either offers good news or presents the Word of God. Homiletical exegesis allows scripture to speak and offer good news appropriate to the context of the people and to the contents of the sermon, whether biblical expository or topical. The step-by-step process for homiletical exegesis for good news sermons provided in Appendix A may be used as a working document by preachers who offer sermons that fit the congregation to whom they are preaching.

IDENTIFICATION OF GOOD NEWS

The process of naming the good news is similar for both biblical expository and topical sermons: unearthing or revealing the evidence of divine grace that speaks to the situation of the hearers. Although the word "gospel"—translated as "good news"—is associated generally with Jesus Christ as fulfillment of the messianic promise, the preacher should resist the temptation to read Jesus into the Old Testament, especially because the word gospel in its generic meaning as good news can be applied legitimately to the whole Bible. In a recent class, several students assured me that in their denominations, it would be anathema not to end every sermon by naming Jesus Christ, whether or not their preaching text had come from the New Testament. This challenged me to find a way to move First Testament sermons into the Second Testament in a way that maintained the integrity of the interpretative process.

While the great good news is our redemption through Jesus Christ, there is always available good news that is representative of the enabling grace of God in the lives of the people of God. Likewise, the grace of God is not a concept that came into being with the apostolic church but was present and operating from the beginning of human history. Thus, exegeting each biblical text for good news means beginning with the theological understanding that the nature of God is above all one of grace. In a similar way, regardless of one's theological stance or the particular divine attribute that one affirms, the basic foundation of theology is the goodness of God. In any context or theological position, this is good news and is the foundation on which all authentic Christian doctrines and practices stand. However, the preacher must not lose sight of the fact that the sermon is not preached in a vacuum, but to a living congregation. Therefore, the context is the beginning point in identifying the need for good news from the sermon. Thus, the action of applying the good news to the congregation is the same for both biblical expository and topical sermons. Originally, I recommended making the discernment of good news from the text the first step in the process. However, it very quickly became clear that in order for the good news to be relevant to the hearers, the preacher needed to make an analysis of the congregation's situation the first in the series of steps leading to the determination and application of good news. Only then could the sermon encourage actions of Christian discipleship by the congregation. These steps may help to identify and apply the good news in both types of sermons:

1. ANALYSIS OF THE CONGREGATION
   - Consider the situation of the congregation; what they are feeling.
   - Determine the need that might guide the style and content of the sermon.
   - Identify the goal that would facilitate Christian discipleship in the hearers.
   - Develop a Sermon Purpose Statement using the following format (see Chapter 1):
     - (Congregational) Situation: *In view of...*
     - (Pastoral) Goal: *to experience...*
     - (Sermonic) Means: *by means of...*
2. CHOOSING THE SERMONIC STYLE: BIBLICAL EXPOSITORY OR TOPICAL
   - The choice of sermonic style, whether biblical expository or topical, is identified in the Sermon Purpose Statement.
   - Approach the biblical text or topic with prayerful expectation of finding good news.
   - Allow the Holy Spirit free rein in revealing the divine presence.
3. FINDING THE THEOLOGICAL MEANING
   - What does the text or topic say about God and the divine/human relationship?
   - Connect the revelation of the divine biblically and/or theologically with the congregational situation.
   - Identify the divine action that speaks of human transformation.

4. NAMING THE GOOD NEWS
   - Using the biblical text or theological representation of the topic, develop a Good News Statement using the following format (see Chapter 1):
     - subject is God (Christ/Holy Spirit)
     - verb is the transformative action of God in human life
     - predicate is the human result of divine/human interaction
   - Test the Good News Statement with the contents or background of the scripture passage or the theological representation to verify that it represents human transformation or empowerment for discipleship.
5. DEVELOPING A DISCIPLESHIP MESSAGE STATEMENT
   - Ask the "so-what?" question of the good news to determine the applicability of the good news of the text to the context of the hearers.
   - Create a Discipleship Message Statement that names the action of Christian discipleship that the good news empowers or facilitates.

An explanation of this process and its three-step exercise are included in chapter 1 in the section entitled "The Importance of Naming Good News in the Sermon."

HOMILETIC EXEGESIS OF THE TEXT OR TOPIC

The interpretive process of homiletical exegesis seeks to unearth the elements of the biblical text or the topic that are critical to developing and offering good news in the sermon. For the biblical expository sermon, the activity of interpretation is generally located in a single text from which the preacher has identified and extracted good news that speaks to the present context. The topical sermon necessitates interpreting the topic to determine its applicability for the moment of preaching first, then interpreting the biblical text or texts to ensure their appropriateness to the topic and to each other. To avoid inappropriate proof-texting, critically interpreting the biblical texts used in preaching the topic is particularly important.

Biblical interpretation allows the text to be heard in its own language and its own images to be seen. Such exegesis brings to light important nuances in the text, and through it the preacher delves as deeply as possible into the biblical record to determine its meaning and focus historically on as many time periods as are relevant for applying it to the present. Some of the most common methods of biblical interpretation are:[6]

- Historical critical method uses textual criteria, engaging the text in its original language, and looks at the historical background, the literary context, and the form and function of the text in the ideology of the ancient world. This method is descriptive, not theological.
- Literary criticism looks at the way in which the form and construction of the text shapes its meaning. Whether the form is identifiable as narrative, saga, myth, legend, historical narrative, dialogue, parable, or some other form, literary criticism addresses the question of its interpretation for theological understanding.
- Form criticism considers the intrinsic shape or form of the text. It is approached by identifying the genre of literature in order to determine the original purpose of the text and its underlying layers of theological meaning.
- Redaction criticism looks at the way in which the redactor as editor used the text to express theological beliefs. This method is historical and is focused on determining the author's purpose in writing the text in order to unearth its meaning and purpose in scripture.

However, while they may use any of these methodologies in the interpretive process, the preacher as homiletician is helped more by a combination of these methods that focuses more on the application of the biblical text(s) to the congregation's context. Exegetically, while the preacher concentrates on learning about the text in its biblical context, they should consider closely the need of the congregation and include in the sermon only those elements of the text that bear directly on the contemporary concern that the sermon addresses. The following is an example of interpretive material applicable to the texts of Matthew 9:35–38 and Jeremiah 29:1, 4–7, based on the sermon purpose, the Good News and Discipleship Message Statements developed in chapter 1:[7]

> Matthew 9:35–38
> 35 Then Jesus went about all the cities and villages, teaching in their synagogues, and proclaiming the good news of the king-
> dom, and curing every disease and every sickness. 36 When he
> saw the crowds, he had compassion for them, because they were harassed and helpless, like sheep without a shepherd. 37 Then he
> said to his disciples, "The harvest is plentiful, but the laborers are
> few; 38 therefore ask the Lord of the harvest to send out laborers
> into his harvest."

- Sermon Purpose Statement: *In view of* the congregation's feeling of insecurity and fear because of the violence in their community, I want the people *to experience* the assurance of God's presence and protection, *by means of a* biblical sermon containing stories of God's care and protection in scripture and in the present.
- Good News Statement: *Christ restores us to wholeness of life.*
- Response to the "so what?" question: So that we can live full and abundant lives.
- Discipleship Message Statement: *Live confidently through the assurance of Christ's presence in your life.*
- Homiletical exegesis (summarized): Verse 35 is a summary statement that marks a transition in Jesus' ministry between the healing miracles recorded in the previous chapter and the charge to the disciples. This one verse summarizes the work that Jesus has been about as he accomplishes those tasks for which he says he came as Luke (4:16–20) describes it. Matthew's language is specific to belief in Jesus as the Messiah, the true shepherd of the people. His gospel is believed

to have been written to instruct the church community in their own faith. His church had carried out an unsuccessful mission to the Jews and he no longer saw these uncommitted persons as potential disciples but rather as harassed and helpless, being misled by synagogue leaders. He understood that the present and future of the church was dependent on non-Jews—Gentiles—and needing leadership in the church community to spread the message of Christ. The text is a narrative composed by its author and based on material adapted from the Gospel of Mark. The story is designed for reading to the whole church community and reminds them of Jesus' compassion—not condemnation—for Israel. The text is appropriate to the present congregation particularly because of their present feelings of fear and insecurity because of the violence in their community (sheep without a shepherd) and their need for the compassionate and healing touch of Christ.

Jeremiah 29:1, 4–7

[1] These are the words of the letter that the prophet Jeremiah sent
from Jerusalem to the remaining elders among the exiles, and to
the priests, the prophets, and all the people, whom Nebuchadnezzar had taken into exile from Jerusalem to Babylon. [4] Thus
says the LORD of hosts, the God of Israel, to all the exiles whom
I have sent into exile from Jerusalem to Babylon: [5] Build houses
and live in them; plant gardens and eat what they produce. [6] Take
wives and have sons and daughters; take wives for your sons, and
give your daughters in marriage, that they may bear sons and
daughters; multiply there, and do not decrease. [7] But seek the welfare of the city where I have sent you into exile, and pray to the
LORD on its behalf, for in its welfare you will find your welfare.

- Good News Statement: *God directs us in our times of fear and uncertainty.*
- Message Statement: *Trust God to guide and support you in every situation.*

- Homiletical exegesis (summarized): This is part of a prophetic oracle presented as a letter from Jeremiah to the exiles that have been deported to Babylon. This portion of the letter has a distinct message. It reminds the exiles that God is the one responsible for sending them into exile and advises the exiles to accept their fate and make the best of their situation. The situation may speak of God's anger at their betrayal of the covenant, and their redemption lies in their ability not only to come to terms with their situation, but also to do good in the place of their captivity. It rests on the assurance of God's presence with them even in their captivity and invites them to be part of the blessing of God in a foreign land. The prophetic voice with which Jeremiah speaks to the exiles brings a message that is difficult to hear given the nationalistic nature of the people. It calls the people back to their covenantal relationship with Yahweh (pray), even in the midst of the devastation of their lives caused by their exile from Jerusalem. Instead of prayers of deliverance from Babylon, they are instructed (by God) to intercede on behalf of their captor (Babylon), which speaks of God's presence and direction even in the times when it seems that God is far away. The text offers to present-day people the reminder and assurance that whether their suffering is self-imposed or caused by issues beyond their control, God is present with the people of God in their times of spiritual and physical suffering (exile). Further, regardless of the circumstances, God offers a word to guide our lives when we are uncertain and fearful and feel as though we are exiled from God's empowering presence.

The selection of interpretive material for use in the sermon is based directly on the focus of the good news. The choice of material to be included in the sermon hinges on both the good news of the sermon and the discipleship message to be delivered to the people. It is not intended to show the entire history or meaning of the selected text, the section of scripture from which it is taken, or the biblical book of which it is a part.

The preacher's focus is determined by the intersection of text and context with respect to its contents as good news and a message that is directive for Christian discipleship.

If the sermon is topical, the preacher interprets the topic to determine whether it fits the context of the life of the congregation theologically, doctrinally, practically, or liturgically. The preacher may begin by addressing one of the doctrines of the church or a particular aspect of an established Christian practice. What is important is that the topic must be specific enough to connect directly with the hearers as individuals. For example, the church may be involved in a stewardship campaign and the pastor may choose to preach on the topic of Christian service as a way of encouraging the members to recognize their gifts and the purpose of their gifts in the life and work of the church. For good news preaching, the preacher begins by addressing two questions of each topic:

- What is the good news that emanates from the topic?
- Does the good news of the topic offer an appropriate message to the situation of the hearers?

For example, on the topic of Christian service, the preacher may focus on the Holy Spirit as the source of the gifts that enable one's service, thereby helping hearers to understand that their gifts are not of their own creation and that they are given by God for a specific purpose, namely, for the building up of the church. Applying a theological framework to the questions allows the preacher to determine the credibility of the topic. Additionally, given that each topic must be supported by appropriate biblical texts, there must also be appropriate biblical interpretation for these supporting texts. The following questions (applied to the topic of Christian service) facilitate this theological investigation:

1. Is the topic theologically sound?

   Most preachers identify with a particular theological position and are likely to choose a topic that fits that position. In preparing to address the topic, the preacher is helped by investigating other theological positions that may bring light to appropriate treatment of the topic. (Christ calls his disciples to be of service in the kingdom of God.)

2. Is the topic representative of Christian tradition, doctrine, or practice?

   Generally topical sermons address some aspect of Christianity, such as tradition, doctrine, or practice. Unfortunately, this does not guarantee that the topic is representative of an acceptable belief or form of Christian discipleship. The history and use of the topic across Christendom help to determine its usefulness in guiding the congregation in their discipleship. (There is a recognized tradition of missional service in the Christian church in the name of Christ.)

3. Is the topic appropriate to biblical history and tradition?

   Since scripture is foundational to all sermons, it is important that biblical reference be readily available for inclusion in the sermon. There may be several and differing positions on the topic in the Bible. Applying the particular aspect of the topic for preaching will help guide the selection of biblical references. (There are several examples of persons dedicated to Christian service recorded in the New Testament, especially in Acts of the Apostles; for example, Dorcas [Acts 9:36–42] and Lydia [Acts 16:13–15].)

4. Is the topic doctrinally appropriate?

   Even when a congregation calls itself nondenominational, it is directed by commonly held Christian doctrines and mores. The traditions common to Christianity provide a measure for determining the appropriateness of the topic beyond specific denominational or congregational beliefs or practices. (The content or measure of Christian service as developed in the sermon differs according to the particular context but has common understanding in Christian history and practice. This may include the work of preachers, teachers, evangelists, missionaries, or other ministries and workers in the church.)

5. Are there past experiences with this topic that may impact its hearing?

   Pastoral wisdom guides the selection and approach to addressing the topic in the particular context. The experience of members is only one aspect of this investigation. Concern for the experience of the wider community, for society in general, and even for the way the topic has been addressed historically also helps determine how suitable the topic is for preaching. The current understanding, history, and practice of service in the congregation will help direct the content of "Christian service" expounded in the sermon. The ministry areas of the church, both past and present, provide information and direction on the types of service applicable to the needs of the congregation that may be presented in the sermon.

HOMILETICAL EXEGESIS OF THE CONGREGATION

The subject and the necessity for analysis of the congregation was introduced in Chapter 1, where I focused on creating the Sermon Purpose Statement. This chapter expands on the necessity, purpose, and method of engaging in focused analysis on the congregation for the purpose of preaching good news. In effect, in the same way that the preacher must exegete the biblical text and the topic in preparation for developing the sermon, so too must the preacher give focused attention to the context, the people, and their situation as individuals. They must understand the community of Christian believers in order to identify and offer good news that connects with and enriches their lives. By taking time to consider the congregation, the preacher is better able to frame the good news in such a way that people in the pews can connect with it. Taking time to address the specific needs of the people will yield its own rewards in the response of the people.

Every congregation expects and is entitled to receive the good news of the gospel that is more than generic in Christian content and that connects with the realities of their life. Homiletic exegesis of the congregation requires the preacher to be aware of the situations that exist within the life of the congregation and beyond into the community and even nationally and globally. However, the preacher should avoid the temptation of speaking to those situations through the sermonic text. Their awareness must focus on the congregation's response to those situations and the prevailing emotions or feelings that members are experiencing. What is important is that the preacher maintains the focus of the message on the good news of the gospel, whether addressed through a text or topic, and its essential role in the formation of Christian discipleship, with the expectation that the congregation will respond in different and new ways to each message.

The congregation's level of biblical literacy, their knowledge and understanding of scripture, and their theological stance have a significant impact on the way that they will hear and receive the good news and respond to the message of the sermon. How the people understand God, the church, and their specific congregation are as important as the culture of their community, their social and political realities. The level of activity and participation in the life and witness of the church also affects the congregation's hearing of good news and directly correlates to their response as Christian disciples. For example, in relation to the topical sermon on Christian service, if in addition to preaching about it, the pastor offers a study on the topic that showcases biblical examples of service to Christ and the church, this will help the congregation to receive the message more deeply and strengthen the invitation to give their service to the church.

The situation of the preaching moment, whether the sermon is for a regular worship service or a special event in the life of the congregation, also has significance for preaching good news, and the expectations of the congregation vary depending on the type of worship service and its place in the liturgical life of the congregation. In addition, the relationship between the preacher and congregation, whether it is ongoing or just a single occasion, makes a difference in how the sermonic message is received. At times, a visiting preacher may be more successful in addressing a difficult matter or preaching a difficult message to the congregation than the assigned pastor. Congregational dynamics, which involve the issue of leadership—both laity and clergy—the application of denominational polity, the structure of committees and groups, and the relationship of age-level groups all play a part in shaping the context for preaching and enabling the hearers to receive and respond to the message of good news.

Given that the congregation is generally part of an immediate community, part of a wider society, a nation and a global world, and given the prevalence of information through news reports, social media and other sources, this will undoubtedly have an impact on the members of the congregation. Since it is unlikely that the preacher will have been trained formally in social analysis, a pastoral approach may yield a clearer picture of the congregational community and a deeper understanding of their joys and concerns. Further, the pastor must recognize their place in the community and the different roles they may represent. It is certain that their presence and participation in the life of the community has a (hopefully positive) impact on the overall life and working of the congregation. Homiletical exegesis of the congregation and its communal life as the body of Christ may provide the level of understanding of the community's situation that facilitates the structure, content and presentation of sermonic good news that is empowering for the congregation. Whether the process of homiletical exegesis is undertaken for a biblical expository or a topical sermon, the preacher benefits from following a systematic approach of contextual exegesis with specific guidelines and questions for interpreting the biblical text for preaching, and that includes the analysis of the preaching context.

A PROCESS FOR EXEGETING THE BIBLICAL EXPOSITORY SERMON[8]

While I do not intend to offer an expansive presentation on the academic requirements of either biblical interpretation or congregational analysis, I have found the following steps in this process to be an effective approach to homiletical exegesis; however, it assumes the preacher's familiarity with common methodologies of biblical interpretation. The process is facilitated by a list of questions, included in appendix B, that are directed to retrieving the necessary information. These suggestions help the preacher engage the process and are not rigid rules to be followed without question.

1. DEFINE THE PREACHING CONTEXT
   - Identify the social, cultural, theological and doctrinal situation of the preaching context.
   - Consider the current issues in the life of the congregation that may need to be addressed.

- Identify broader social, cultural, political and economic issues beyond the immediate congregation that need to be addressed.

2. MEET THE TEXT
   - Approach the text with expectation. Be open and prepared to hear something new from the text.
   - Read the text with a listening attitude. Read the text aloud several times, each with a different emphasis if possible.
   - Engage as many senses as possible and give your emotions free rein. Listen for the good news that arises from the text. Listen for its message on discipleship. Listen for words that seem significant.
3. LOCATE THE TEXT BIBLICALLY
   - Establish the boundaries of the text. Does the passage seem connected or disconnected from the surrounding text?
   - Determine the literary form and how it affects the meaning of the text. Identify and determine the significance of its authorship and placement in the greater corpus.
   - Establish the plain sense of the text, that is, what is the surface meaning of the text? What do the words themselves seem to say? Does everything in the text make sense? Look for changes in setting, characters, and theme.
   - How does the meaning of particular words or phrases help establish the meaning of the text? Note items from an introduction to the book that might be important for interpreting this passage.
   - Check whether this is a layered passage, that is, is this a narrative, is this a single story, or are there multiple layers of story or plot written into or hidden in the text?
4. LOCATE THE TEXT HISTORICALLY
   - Determine the historical setting of the text. Ask the introductory questions: Who was the author? Where was the text written? When was it written? For what purpose was it written?
   - Identify the biblical history. How many biblical periods affect the meaning of this text? Parables, for example, are presented

according to the context of the gospel writer but are referential to Jesus' time when the parable was told originally.

- Determine the author's intention in writing this passage to a particular audience. Is the author trying to confirm or challenge the views of the reader?
- Establish the dynamics that were important to the community to whom the text was written. What are the social, cultural, political, and religious realities that affected the way in which the text was written and presented to the original hearers?

5. ENGAGE THE LITERARY FORM AND CONTENTS

- Identify the form of the text and its influence on how the text is read. Does its form—as narrative/non-narrative, saga, myth, legend, historical narrative, scholastic writing, dialogue, law, prophecy, parable, or other—hold intrinsic meanings for the interpretation of the text?
- What are the bridge words that move the message of the text along and how do they give particular meaning to the sequencing of the action contained in the text?
- Which words have history that bears further examination or requires additional research into their origins?
- Does the form of the text offer or dictate a particular model for the sermon?

6. ENGAGE THE TEXT IMAGINATIVELY

- Interrogate the text using your senses and emotions, considering how the text was originally heard and received and how much of that feeling would apply to the present hearers.
- Allow the theological, existential, experiential issues you identified to focus your interpretation of the text for the preaching context. Consider how the text was heard by the original audience.
- Do the biblical images present in the text suggest appropriate imagery for the present?

- Use your imagination to connect the text with elements such as art, nature, events and people. Identify at least three elements that help to bring the text to life.

7. CONTEXTUALLY INTERPRET THE TEXT
   - How much of the historical atmosphere is necessary for the congregation to relate to the text.
   - Are there parallels to be made between the context of the text and the current situation of the congregation.
   - What ideological issues are raised for modern readers by or over against the text?

8. CONTEXTUALIZE THE TEXT FOR GOOD NEWS FOR THE PRESENT
   - Connect the text with the present. How can the social, cultural, political, and religious situations of the text compare to or impact the present?
   - How does this text achieve significance for the present congregation?
   - How can the good news contained in the text have significance for the present congregation?
   - What contemporary assumptions influence the way this passage is read, for good or for ill?

This approach is deliberately simple in form and does not require knowledge of original biblical languages. However, preachers who are versed in established areas of biblical interpretation can do additional work to deepen their understanding of the text and connect it more closely with the context of the sermon. The substance of this homiletical exegesis helps to inform the preacher's understanding of the meaning and use of the text in preaching. It helps the preacher to determine any possible connection between the congregation for whom the text was written originally or to identify an inherent disconnect that must be overcome in order to make the passage relevant. This exegetical work helps the preacher to consider whether the original readers or hearers would have been comforted, offended or challenged by this text, and what expectations the readers might have had each step of the way through the passage.

Although commentaries are generally helpful in homiletical exegesis, preachers should engage with the texts critically before turning to commentaries. Otherwise, the preacher does a disservice to her or his opportunity and ability to allow the text to speak to the specific context of preaching and to the preacher's own situation in proclaiming good news. The purpose of commentaries is to increase one's knowledge of the text and provide depth and support for one's own ideas. However, it is important that such documentation be selected carefully so that it is representative of current scholarship. Moreover, in the case of the Bible, supplemental literature should give careful attention to each book separately, in addition to an overview of the section of biblical writing in which it belongs, and should treat biblical periods, genres of biblical literature, themes, and history separately and with integrity.

In addition to Bible commentaries, a good study Bible may also be helpful in providing simple background material that can give insight and assist in framing the text for preaching. My personal preference is *The New Interpreter's Bible: A Commentary in Twelve Volumes* (Nashville: Abingdon Press, 1994–1998) and *The New Interpreter's Study Bible: New Revised Standard Version with The Apocrypha* (Nashville: Abingdon Press, 2003); however, I believe it would be unethical to make specific suggestions for either a study Bible or Bible commentary.

Additionally, there are online sources that provide reliable material that is useful for developing and preaching good news sermons. There are several academic and scholarly organizations that provide such information, and seminary librarians are generally also a good source. The checklist of questions provided in appendix B includes questions for both interpreting the text and connecting the text with the context of preaching. It may be used each time you do exegesis for a biblical expository sermon on any biblical text.

A PROCESS FOR EXEGETING THE TOPICAL SERMON

Even a topical sermon finds its foundation in a biblical text, although the interpretation centers not so much on the meaning of one text, but in the application and meaning of the topic for the context of preaching. The purpose for addressing any topic is always to offer good news to the congregation. The good news and the message arising from the topic together are intended to impact and support the discipleship of individuals and the congregation. Each text used in unpacking and relating the topic to the congregation should be exegeted, but there is usually a major text that is chosen as foundational to the topic. The foundational text on which the topic rests requires interpretation to connect it with the preaching context. An understanding of the role of each of the multiple texts used to support the topic is necessary but they do not require rigorous exegesis. Often, topical preaching is engaged as part of a sermon series. In such cases, it is important to establish the boundaries of the topic, to identify the wider, general topic that you intend to address and break it apart into smaller, more manageable pieces by creating an outline of topic and subtopics, then narrow and frame the scope of the topic of each sermon.

The process outlined in this section, and the list of questions provided in appendix C, are suggestions only and are not to be considered prescriptive for topical exegesis. Please note the similarities in the processes of exegesis for biblical expository and for topical sermons. Homiletical exegesis begins with the definition of the preaching context regardless of the style of the sermon.

1. DEFINE THE PREACHING CONTEXT
   - Identify the social, cultural, theological and doctrinal situation of the preaching context.
   - Consider the current issues in the life of the congregation that may need to be addressed.
   - Identify broader social, cultural, political and economic issues beyond the immediate congregation that need to be addressed.
2. MEET THE TOPIC
   - The purpose for addressing any topic is always to offer good news to the congregation.

- The good news and the message arising from the topic together are intended to impact and support the discipleship of individuals and the congregation.

3. ESTABLISH THE BOUNDARIES OF THE TOPIC
   - If this sermon is part of a series, create an outline consisting of the general topic and the sub-topics arising from it, then verify that the flow of topics fits an appropriate pattern, or that subtopics are presented correctly to reach a desired goal.
   - Verify the purpose or goal of the sermon and the relevance of the topic to the situation of the congregation.

4. NARROW AND FRAME THE SCOPE OF THE TOPIC
   - Topical sermons are generally based on theology, Christian doctrine, or Christian practice, which are open to broad interpretation biblically and theologically. For preaching, the scope of the topic moves from the general to the specific.
   - Using the outline of topic and subtopics created earlier in the process, select the specific topic for preaching.
   - Develop a similar outline for the preaching topic (previously subtopic) that lists key points for preaching that exposes the topic to the congregation.
   - Develop three or four that may be presented in the sermon.

5. CONNECT THE TOPIC WITH THE BIBLE
   - A topic may originate from a biblical text, or the text may be selected based on the topic. In either case this text should be considered foundational to the topic. Exegete this text fully as for a biblical expository sermon.
   - Different texts may be connected with the individual points to be made in preaching the topic. These texts are considered as secondary to the foundational text.
   - Exegete any secondary texts sufficiently to verify that they are representative of the meaning of the foundational text and of the preaching topic.

6. SITUATE THE TEXT THEOLOGICALLY AND DOCTRINALLY
   - Verify that the approach and the interpretation of the topic meets accepted theology.
   - The subject of the topic must also be in accord with accepted Christian doctrines and with the denominational traditions of the congregation.
7. LOCATE THE TOPIC HISTORICALLY AND CONTEXTUALLY
   - Consider and review the ways in which the topic has been approached historically and what scripture texts other preachers have used to address this topic.
   - Investigate the way in which the topic and the texts used to support it have functioned in the church at large and in the present congregation.
   - Locate the topic within the situation of the congregation. Restate the purpose for preaching on the particular topic.
8. DETERMINE THE SIGNIFICANCE OF THE TOPIC FOR THE PRESENT
   - Check the relevance of the topic for the context of preaching and whether it will achieve significance for the present congregation.
   - Identify the good news from scripture that relates to the application of the topic in the congregation and ensure the message of the sermon fits the substance of the topic.
   - Consider the relevance of the topic to congregational, societal, or world issues and its impact on or relationship to Christian discipleship.

In exegeting the topical sermon, avoid the temptation of using so much of the biblical material that the sermon becomes biblical expository in form and content. The topical sermon is representative of a Christian doctrine or practice or theological position, and the good news of the sermon leads to a call to discipleship within the context of that doctrine, practice or theology, but also supports the reality of divine grace as transformative for living in the present. The checklist of questions provided in appendix C may be used each time you do exegesis for a topical sermon or any topic for preaching. It is a useful guide and not to be considered as the definitive method for exegeting a topic for preaching.

three

Theological Constructs and Constraints in Forming Good News Sermons

On one of the first evenings of my Theology of Ministry I class in seminary, a visiting British minister, John Vincent,[1] shared his thoughts on theology for ministry. He said, "The best theologian for you is you." He clarified his words by explaining that only the individual can say exactly who or what God is for that person. Theology is defined as the study of God, and our theology speaks of our understanding of who God is for us individually and who or what God is for the world. The theological integrity of the sermon depends on the preacher's theology—how he or she understands God. How each of us experiences God is as different, as unique as our fingerprints. What we preach reveals our understanding of and relationship with God.

Fred Craddock, speaking of the situation of preaching, believes that each preacher needs to reassess not only one's role as a preacher but also "one's view of the congregation as the people of God, one's understanding of whether the sermon is the preacher's."[2] In other words, while the theology of the preacher has a significant impact on the contents and the preaching of the sermon, it is preached in the midst of people, each of whom may have a different understanding of who God is in their life. The people may hold in common aspects of a particular theology, which may or may not be the same as the preacher's, but regardless, they also influence the development, contents, and preaching of the sermon.

This chapter considers the requirements for developing a good news sermon that is theologically sound and congruent with the gospel contained in scripture. It also addresses the question of how the preacher can be sure that the sermon offers a revelation of the God of scripture. While exegesis allows the preacher to look into, behind, and beneath the text to unearth its meaning for the present, the work of biblical interpretation does not uncover the full meaning of God or the Word of God for the life of the people. If the subject of the good news is God, and it is, then it follows that the preacher's understanding of God must include the conviction of grace as a key attribute of God. How does the preacher ensure that the sermon speaks clearly and accurately of the love of God? What safeguards can be put in place to help the preacher develop a sermon that is appropriate to the biblical record of the covenantal love of God? To do so requires that it be constructed with theological accuracy and integrity, particularly with respect to the truth of the love of God for all people.

"As a man thinketh in his heart so is he." That was my father's version of the Proverbs 23:7 text, and as he was wont to do, he used this biblical truism to express his displeasure when one of his children acted in objectionable ways. Applying that sentiment to the theology of the preacher I say: As the preacher believes about God in the heart, so that preacher preaches. A sermon cannot offer good news unless its message gives light to the majesty of God's love and unless it witnesses to the loving presence of God in human life and invites hearers to experience that love and offer their own witness to it through faithful discipleship. This chapter offers insights and exercises that will guide the preacher in developing good news sermons with theological integrity.

A THEOLOGY OF GOOD NEWS

Scripture, as the biblical record of God's interaction in the lives of human persons, is our chief accepted source of the good news. Scripture informs theology. It gives us ways to understand God, as creator, defender, protector, guide, liberator, and whatever attribute of God makes God visible and available to you. Similarly, theology, the study of God and God's relationship to the created world and specifically the people of the world, informs our reading of scripture. Whatever our understanding of God, theology provides the lens through which we read the biblical record and interpret the stories of divine/human interaction recorded in the Bible. As preachers, we are inspired by the stories of the prophets from Moses through Elijah and Elisha, Isaiah and Jeremiah, Amos and Micah, and all the greater and lesser prophets who were mouthpieces for God. Their messages told of God's covenantal love for humanity, whether in affirmation or denouncement of the actions of the people. Through all the words of prophecy ran the thread of divine love that was never diminished by the burden of human sin and thus was always in reality a theology of good news.

A "theology of good news" keeps central the active and ongoing acceptance of God's grace that is above all and through all and in all things for the good of the whole people of God. A theology of good news speaks of God joyfully and invites hearers of the word into the fullness of joy that is the result of divine love. Theology is the source of the words of the good news sermon. There is a symbiotic relationship between theology and scripture. Each informs the other. How God is depicted in the stories of the Bible contributes to the development of one's theology. Often the bedrock of a preacher's theology is the uncritical childhood reading of scripture that defined the nature of God. Bible stories learned in early years often leave an indelible imprint that either hinders the preacher from accepting fully the attribute of grace that is the heart of God for created humanity or enables understanding and acceptance of the unending grace of God for all humanity. If the former, then the preacher may find it difficult to accept that all of scripture is founded on divine grace, that every text may be linked to the grace of God, and that the preacher has the opportunity to offer good news in every sermon.

Paul Scott Wilson also weighs in on the critical nature of good news as a missing element of many sermons. He offers several theological reasons for a change in the way that sermons are created.[3] He notes that the absence of God in our sermons may manifest that "God is missing from the center of our own lives."[4] Unless one's understanding of God includes one's personal experience of the same covenantal love that is the thread that runs through all of scripture, one is unable to witness to that truth with integrity. Even when the preacher understands and accepts the grace of God personally, that theological frame of reference does not appear explicitly when the preacher is not intentional in ensuring that the good news of the sermon is recognizable as such. The love of God created all things to be good; that love redeemed fallen humanity through Jesus Christ; and that same love unstintingly and unwaveringly guides, supports and directs us through the Holy Spirit. Living in and preaching the great love of God comes from a theological understanding of God's transformative, regenerative love—a theology of good news that offers the hearers real good news.

This is a book on preaching, and it does not represent a particular theology. One's theology shapes and is shaped by the preached Word of God, so having a theology of good news for preaching ensures that each sermon offers good news to the hearers. God's grace is active and ongoing, eternally creative and creating, shaping and reshaping fallen humanity into the image of Christ. This ongoing activity of redemption and salvation and the divine/human interaction it necessitates is the good news that brings overflowing life to those who accept and participate in it as a gift of grace. A preacher's theology of good news claims, articulates, and imparts to hearers the reality of the divine covenant.

The following questions will help you assess your own theology of good news:

1: DO YOU HAVE A CLEAR AND UNQUESTIONED UNDERSTANDING OF SCRIPTURE AS THE RECORD OF GOD'S COVENANTAL LOVE FOR HUMANITY?

Beyond the details of history and pseudohistory that comprise the biblical record is the Word of God. Theologically that means that inerrancy is not a prerequisite to the understanding of the real presence of God in history and specifically in the record of those whose lives have been chronicled for posterity. The Judeo-Christian heritage that has been embraced by the church gives substance to divine love that is often misunderstood, misrepresented, and unfathomable. That love portrayed in scripture is the fulfillment of covenant, made and kept by God, accepted and broken across time by human beings. And it is the biblical witness of that unbroken covenant that leaps from the pages of antiquity and that the preacher must embrace and engage in order to give voice to the good news that it offers. Although the scripture text may lend itself to good news preaching, the authentic witness of scripture comes not from simply preaching the words, but from the preacher's application of her or his theological stance, one that is directed and supported by the preacher's belief in the good news of divine grace.

In studying scripture, the preacher must look beyond the immediacy of translated words, and retold and reframed stories, to recognize, understand, and witness the presence and work of God in the situations of the biblical stories. This requires an act of faith. By faith the preacher is moved to accept the unfathomable and to believe the unexplainable as it applies to the love of God for all people. The words of scripture retold by preachers and by the church may even offer contradictions in the record of events and places and people. It is nevertheless the Word of God, "useful for teaching, for reproof, for correction, and for training in righteousness" (2 Timothy 3:16), and these activities are all requisite to the shaping of one's theology. Accepting the biblical record with the caveat of divine inspiration requires an act of faith.

While scripture may not engender faith, accepting scripture by faith enables the preacher to see more clearly the presence of God in scripture and to give credence appropriately to the messages of God's love that are woven into the texts of scripture. By faith the preacher stands not simply to relate the stories of old, but through these timeworn yet timeless stories to call the people and to join with them in becoming active participants in the divine/human drama that witnesses the grace of God. Scripture is thus a sustaining word for the preacher who is empowered to share that faith in the good news offered through the sermon.

2: DO YOU EXPERIENCE A SENSE OF JOY WHEN YOU SEE THE EVIDENCE OF GOD'S GRACE IN THE BIBLE?

Many preachers feel a sense of compulsion to call hearers to live fully into their Christian identity, but too many in their disciple-making zeal have resorted to harangue and threats as the way of salvation. Congregations have been beaten up and knocked down by preachers who are filled with a sense of doom because of the state of humanity and the world at large. When that is the worry in the preacher's heart, it is impossible to be joyful or to encourage hearers to experience the joy of God's presence even in the midst of the world's greatest disasters. In other words, not only is there no good news, but the preacher is lost in a morass of death and destruction and has missed the celebration of the overcoming wrought by God's enlivening presence.

Certainly, there are scripture texts that seem to speak of anything but love, joy, and peace, the attributes normally associated with the grace of God. But with careful and authentic interpretation of biblical texts in their historical contexts, one may find the not-so-hidden love of God beneath their obvious and often distressing representation in the record of scripture. The preacher that takes the biblical text only at face value may lose sight of its true meaning in its historical context and use the text inappropriately. What may appear as God's unrepentant anger at the people's fickleness may hide the loving concern that underlies God's severe response to the people's actions.

Similarly, the preacher who looks at the present situation and compares it to the biblical record that depicts the punishment of an angry God is inclined to miss the moments of divine grace that are interwoven in the text and that served to bring the people back into right relationship with God and with each other. But the preacher who is driven by a theology of good news will search beneath the words of the text to discover the treasure trove of God's love that is ever present in divine actions. Such a discovery calls forth joyful praise and thanksgiving for the inestimable love of God.

3: IS YOUR RELATIONSHIP WITH SCRIPTURE IN DEVELOPING THE SERMON AN AFFIRMING EXPERIENCE?

The work of developing the sermon for preaching invites the preacher to experience and invest in a sincere and serious relationship with God, with the people of God, and with scripture, the Word of God. The preacher's relationship with the words of scripture helps to increase the knowledge and understanding of the presence of God and ultimately informs and shapes the preacher's theology in a systematic way. Studying the biblical stories sharpens knowledge and increases wisdom about what it means to be constant recipients of the grace of God. Thus, the text shapes the preacher's theology, and the systemization of the preacher's theology influences how the preacher proclaims the good news.

The preacher's experience with scripture, specifically for developing the sermon, not only involves delving into the words and the underlying meaning of scripture texts but requires also that the preacher maintain communication with God throughout the process to ensure that the words of the sermon represent the Word of God for the people. The preacher's ongoing conversation with God as it pertains to scripture must be for the purpose of discerning the Word of God that arises from the particular text, for the specific event of preaching. How the preacher experiences this influences the way in which the preacher approaches scripture as the repository of good news.

Each event of preaching offers an opportunity to search or wrestle with the scripture text for the good news that it contains. The good news preacher approaches the text with the expectation of finding good news, and when that venture meets with success it affirms both the divine/human dialogue of prayer and the faith that caused the preacher to undertake the search in the first place. The preacher thus becomes a witness to scripture as a record of God's love for humanity and celebrates the success through the words of the sermon and by subsequent forays into the Bible for the purpose of finding and preaching good news.

BIBLICAL THEOLOGY: FINDING GRACE

Paul Scott Wilson, in his contribution to the festschrift in honor of David Buttrick, notes Buttrick's concern with the influence of biblical theology on homiletics. Both homileticians considered the distance between the Bible and the present to be detrimental to the preaching task, and one particular area of their concern is the ability of the preacher to interpret the biblical text appropriately for hearers in the present. As Wilson named it, in order to reconnect the Bible and preaching, "the focus must be on helping preachers to move from the biblical text to the contemporary situation and on recasting theology in the present."[5] Biblical theology not only sheds light on the meaning of the text, it reveals God's initiating, creating presence; frames the need for and the substance of God's redemption as the offset to human sin; and gives substance to the sustaining presence of God in human endeavor that originates from the heart of divine love. It is the Word of God for the people of God that calls forth a doxological response from people and preacher together.

Biblical theology digs into the historical record of God contained in scripture to identify how believers understand who God is. There is no single doctrinal position that is central or uniform with respect to biblical theology. In fact, the very resources that have been engaged in the effort to make the meaning of scripture clearer and more accessible for preaching have often run counter to the need of homiletics that "seeks to render the Word of God in a manner that is faithful to the biblical witness, scholarship, and tradition, yet is specific to our time."[6] In that sense, the preacher undertakes the task of biblical theology in order to help to connect text and context so that the claims of the sermon are in accord with the claims of the scripture text on which it stands. Biblical interpretation meets theological understanding as the substance of biblical theology for preaching.

Good news preaching offers grace from each text. Biblical theology reveals the grace that resides in the text. The following questions may help unearth that grace in the text:

WHAT DOES THE TEXT SAY ABOUT GOD OR THE ACTION OF GOD?

Since a significant portion of the biblical record does not speak openly of God's love in action, it requires an interpretive process to unearth God's activity of grace or even God's presence in the context of historical events. It is important that the preacher not rush to name God as principal when the action seems to give evidence of the mark of the divine. An example of such misrepresentation may be seen in the parables, where God is often assigned the role of master or king as in the parable of the wicked tenants, or as father as in the parable of the prodigal son. To authentically unearth the divine action, the preacher must carefully deconstruct the historical realities surrounding the text. The purpose of that task is to verify that the preacher's theological conclusions are both accurate and appropriate.

DOES THE CLAIM OF DIVINE GRACE ARISE FROM THE CONTENTS OF THE BIBLICAL TEXT?

The unbroken thread throughout all of scripture is covenant. God makes and keeps covenant with humanity. Human beings make or agree to a covenantal relationship with God and constantly and consistently break the covenant. Divine grace operates within that covenant and speaks more clearly about divine love than about human desire. Thus, in determining the claim of grace, the preacher must consider carefully the true meaning of the text and decipher its contribution to the people's understanding and acceptance of the unbounded love of God. The language of scripture must flow into the present in a way that enables the Word of God to be recognized in the language of the people of faith.

The preacher's theology is shaped not only by scripture, but also by the church and by society at large. Over the centuries of its existence, the church has worked deliberately to define its theology. Differences based on the understanding of scripture have resulted in differing doctrines and denominational splits, which may have a direct influence not only on the reading and understanding of scripture, but also on the preacher's understanding of the divine/human relationship. A theology of good news for all people, which Jesus declared as his mission, helps the preacher to avoid the trap of categorizing the hearers either as the chosen of God and exclusive recipients of God's favor, or the condemned who are beyond the grace of God.

The community, subject to the particular theology of their denomination, may resist hearing the good news of unfettered grace for all people, but the preacher must, in turn, resist the seductive pull of being among the chosen and allow the witness of scripture to stand as proof to the nature of the grace of God given freely to all people. Likewise, faced with a text of scripture that seems to discriminate and therefore segregate humanity into selective groups, the preacher is challenged to resist the temptation to speak so narrowly to the present congregation that the words of the sermon take the hearers outside of the beloved community. Every sermon must offer good news that is authentic to the eternal covenant that defines the love of God for the whole of humanity.

Good news preaching requires language that works as a filter between the words of scripture and the unrelenting cries of the people. Symbols of the Christian faith such as creation, sin, redemption, new birth, the community in Christ, and eternal life are encompassed in the good news sermon because they are the core of scripture, the essence of the divine/human relationship, and the reality of God's covenant of love in action in the lives of individuals and the community. The preacher cannot dismiss one in preference to the other, because they all represent the core of Christianity and therefore of Christian preaching. This requires that the preacher have a defined homiletical theology that works to determine the contents of the sermon such that it brings to light the active presence of the divine in the selection and shaping of the sermonic message that will be brought to the gathered congregation.

HOMILETICAL THEOLOGY

I define homiletical theology as the connection between one's understanding of the place of the divine applied specifically to the task of developing and preaching the sermon to the people gathered as the church. The preacher's homiletic theology, whether acknowledged or not, determines how that preacher not only engages biblical theology to reveal divine activity in the biblical text, and how that text is interpreted for the life of the people. It also impacts the way in which the preacher recognizes and accepts the presence and work of the divine as the enabling power in their development of the sermon. As already stated, one's theology speaks of one's understanding of the place of the divine not only in one's life but in the world and in all aspects of human life and endeavors. To speak of a homiletical theology is to build on that foundation in practical ways. It considers the place and action of the divine in enabling the preacher to discern the presence and grace of God in and through the biblical text, particularly texts that are considered problematic or challenging in content or even in their original context. The preacher's homiletical theology influences the shaping of the sermon for effective gospel proclamation in the context of the congregation, even as it helps in the shaping of the preacher as a proclaimer of the gospel. The necessity for offering good news at every event of preaching is the thesis upon which this work is predicated, and understanding one's homiletical theology allows the preacher to sharpen their focus on the presence and work of the divine, most often recognized as the Holy Spirit, as a force that influences the content and the format of the message to be preached in both spiritual and tangible ways. Thus, homiletical theology brings into play the preacher's commitment to ensuring that the presence of God is palpable in both the various tasks required for the creation of the sermon and in the actual words of the sermon.

David Schnasa Jacobsen, in the introduction to his text *Homiletical Theology in Action*, begins with a reference to Karl Barth, who "famously argued that all theology is sermon preparation."[7] Jacobsen's focus in this text, as he names it, was "to demonstrate how various dimensions of homiletical theology, whether made explicit or operating more implicitly, shape the work that preachers do."[8] That claim is representative of the position or understanding that each preacher, in response to the call to participate in the work of proclaiming the gospel, willingly recognizes and intentionally looks to divine action and interaction in their lives and in the process of sermon creation. Where biblical theology speaks to the belief that God is present in the words of scripture and in preparation for preaching, specifically the scripture text(s) used as foundation for the sermon, homiletical theology shines light on the words that will comprise the sermon and the way in which they represent the inspiration of the divine. The words of the sermon arise from the mind of the preacher. They are based in part on the preacher's understanding of the biblical text, but also on how the preacher connects the biblical text(s) with the lives of the people and the understanding that these texts are gifted by the Holy Spirit. Homiletical theology can thus be understood as a highly contextual enterprise that influences the contents of the sermon so that it is congruent with the situation of the hearers of the sermon.

In too many instances, congregations are bombarded with sermonic material that, while taken from scripture, is used in a way that is less than affirming, and may be downright harmful to the hearers. Not long ago, in a conversation on the upcoming lectionary texts, a preacher proudly shared with me the title of the sermon he would preach in the planned service, which he said was inspired by the scripture text and a popular movie that had recently been brought to the public. The title, although he said it was meant to be tongue in cheek, contained a call to hate a certain group of people. In our conversation, the preacher tried to explain that the title was meant to capture the attention of the hearers, but I maintained that as Christians, hate does not belong in our vocabulary, and certainly not in either the title or the contents of a gospel message to the people of God. As Christians, we are called to be harbingers of love and justice in the name of Christ, and the preacher stands in the gap between God and the people, to offer them a word of grace that speaks to Christ's transformative presence in their lives and sustenance for the challenges that they face. The preacher's homiletical theology is a significant element in determining what the sermon offers to the hearers.

Homiletical theology influences the beliefs, practices, and theories that guide and enable the preacher to envision the hoped-for outcome of the sermon and its impact and influence on the lives of the hearers. In effect, homiletical theology as a discipline must influence and impact the efforts that result in the creation of a message that engages the context in which it will be heard, the purpose for which the sermon has been developed, and the goal that the preacher hopes it will attain. In his text, Jacobsen identified three modes of homiletical theology that align in several ways with the generalized definition and understanding of homiletical theology put forward in this text. The modes addressed by the contributors to Jacobsen's text are (1) descriptive, (2) confessional, and (3) analytical.[9] The descriptive mode speaks to my understanding of the need for theological interpretation brought into use by the preacher that arises from the biblical text. It is to a large extent what has already been described in this text as biblical theology. The confessional mode brings into play the preacher's personal theology described in the context of a theology of good news based on the preacher's personal relationship with God and the work of the Holy Spirit in the life of the preacher. The analytical mode refers to the homiletical task required to construct a sermon. This element of sermon preparation involves engaging one's imagination and expanding one's mind to facilitate the work of the Holy Spirit in the life of both preacher and congregation.

As stated earlier in this chapter, the shaping of the preacher's theology is a confluence of scripture, the doctrines of the Christian Church and the preacher's denomination or church affiliation, and the influences of society and prevailing cultures, the development of the preacher's homiletical theology builds on this theological base and adds deeper understanding of the sermon as instructive for helping to develop the Christian life of the people and guiding and encouraging their discipleship in the world. In other words, one's homiletical theology invites and encourages greater attentiveness to the contents of the message such that it enables verification of its fitness for delivery to the gathered congregation. And given the particular focus of this work, it seems appropriate to go even a step further and speak of a homiletical theology of good news.

A HOMILETICAL THEOLOGY OF GOOD NEWS

Admittedly, the definition of this theological construct may be somewhat repetitive of material and ideas put forward earlier in this chapter; however, to my mind, it deserves a brief exposition to bring to the forefront unique characteristics insofar as the Good News Preaching is concerned. A homiletical theology of good news is a key component in the preparatory work of developing the good news sermon. The good news as the active, transformative presence of God in human endeavors is a difficult concept for many of my students to grasp. As a result, many struggle in their effort to define the divine action in ways that recognize that God is always at work making things new, guiding the people in the ways of justice and mercy, and showing forth the active grace of God operating for the good of all people. Indeed, a theology of good news brings to center stage the reality of the active, present, and ongoing grace of God in human life, even in the midst of overwhelming challenges. A preacher faced with the reality of too many of life's challenges may be tempted to join those who wonder at and doubt that God cares about faulty, frail humanity. When that happens, the preacher's sermon, offered as evidence that the preacher is aware of and concerned about the trials of the people's lives, may offer sympathy or empathy for their situation without turning the corner and showing how and where God's activity is offering transformative grace. Having an active homiletical theology of good news can mitigate that desire and call the preacher back to the critical task of offering good news to the people of God.

Where a theology of good news is the source of the good news, a homiletical theology of good news ensures that the good news takes pride of place in the content of the sermon in a way that causes the hearers to rethink the situations that they might have given into as impossible to overcome. The preacher who grounds their work in a homiletical theology of good news will ensure that every sermon offers the hearers the reality of God's love for humanity. The sermons developed under the rubric of a homiletical theology of good news will present God's grace without dismissing the reality of the human situation that necessitated the sermon. When the purpose that the sermon addresses has been brought into play with a homiletical theology of good news, the preacher is able to bring both to light even as they find the necessary means, through the words of the sermon, to make visible the presence and work of God for the good of the people, which is or must be the goal of all preachers and sermons.

Theological adequacy and appropriateness are the mandate of every preacher and every sermon. However, neither requirement can be met fully unless the sermon intentionally and specifically offers good news. In the midst of tragedy and persecution, the ancient writers worked diligently to show that God was present with the people. In times of slavery and exile, of disobedience and unfaithfulness, in persecution and oppression, God was present. That was the message of the prophets and the temple, of synagogue and church worshipers, who all listened for the Word of God from the preachers of their time.

The people of God in this time are still seeking and expecting an authentic word of divine grace from the mouth of today's preachers. The Bible is still the trusted record of divine love in history, and the preacher who stands to declare a message to the church in the name of God does so wisely with awesome fear and through divine grace. Each preacher is constrained in preaching by this reality but is also empowered to construct a sermon that not only speaks of the historical reality of the love of God, but that offers it freely to the present congregation through the words of the sermon. The contents of the sermon, developed from the preacher's theology, created according to the requirements of a homiletical theology of good news, are thus proclaimed as testimonial to the active, empowering love of God. And that is good news preaching.

four

Connecting and Contextualizing the Good News Sermon for Your Congregation

Every sermon is contextual. Sermons are preached to a particular people, at a particular time and place. Preaching that is not contextual creates a void between preacher and people. My personal experience of this occurred when I used an illustration from a popular song by Janet Jackson, an African American pop artist, in a sermon preached to my white upper-middle-class congregation. The illustration was right on target with the content of my sermon, but it missed the mark completely in this community. Contextualizing the sermon requires knowing the social, cultural, theological, and doctrinal norms as well as the experiences of the community past and present. Without this knowledge, the gap between preacher and people, sermon and good news, becomes an ever-widening chasm as the preacher continues preaching above, below, or beyond the people or in a way that is unconcerned or unconnected with their lives.

In this chapter we look at the nature of preaching as contextual and the reason, purpose, and importance of contextualization in preaching. We consider some simple tools that facilitate the creation of sermons that are contextualized to fit and therefore connect with the congregations to whom they are preached. My particular focus is the development of good news that is appropriate to the context of preaching. Preachers are helped in their preaching when they take time to learn about the people to whom they preach. The preacher who arrives in a congregation with the feeling that he or she knows exactly what the people need to hear, and who takes no time to meet and greet the people before preaching to them about their need for better discipleship, does a disservice to the people, to the text, to him- or herself, and to God. Especially in such situations, otherwise good sermons fall flat because a sermon is effective only when it connects with the people. The preached news is not good if it does not reach the people with an appropriate message of God's grace.

CONTEXTUAL GOOD NEWS PREACHING

Contextual preaching allows the content of the sermon to be in accordance with the culture and needs of the congregation. However, at times good news that speaks of grace for all people, including those beyond the congregation, may not initially be considered good news by the hearers of the sermon. A good example of this is a church that has shut its doors and retreated behind those doors because of new people in the community. The preacher who comes to this congregation, learns the culture of separatism, and preaches within those boundaries is neither preaching contextually nor offering good news. On the other hand, if the preacher contextualizes the sermon, it could offer divine grace as a means of addressing and overcoming the fear or other emotions that have caused the prevailing attitude. In doing so, not only does the sermon take account of the congregation's cultural context, but it also offers real good news. In this way the content of good news arises out of the text, and it connects with and addresses the congregation's situation. With these elements meeting together, the sermon earns the title of a contextual good news sermon.

Good news preaching intentionally, appropriately, and explicitly offers the good news of divine grace to the gathered community in a particular time and place. This definition emphasizes both the preacher's responsibility to proclaim good news that is the purpose of every sermon, and the requirement to be intentional in ensuring that the sermon is appropriate to the hearers. Contextualizing the sermon requires that one engage a process of congregational analysis that is concurrent with the work of biblical interpretation. The pastor/preacher who lives with the people on a daily basis must be as intentional about analyzing the congregation for preaching as does the visiting preacher. Life is never static, and although the yesterdays help to inform the present-day moment of preaching, the preacher does well to keep in step with the changes in society, the culture, and the world as well as in the congregation itself, as all these affect the content and shape of the congregation.

Just as the congregation changes physically over time, so too does it change theologically because of the same influences of culture, church, and world that affect the preacher. The congregation's experiences of God-with-us give substance and credibility to their faith and directly affect the theological belief and structure of the church. The preacher who is concerned with the issue of contextualization also recognizes that although there may be a predominant theological position in the congregation, there are generally many theologies that are subordinate to the corporate theology of the group but that are just as influential in shaping the theological context of the community.

Whether it is the substance of the gospel itself, the preacher's struggle with the revelation of the good news, or the ability of the congregation to hear the good news of the sermon, by the preacher's contextualizing the sermon, the good news has a greater chance of reaching the hearers. The contents of scripture and the salvific message of the gospel are often as challenging for Christians as for non-Christians. At times preachers struggle with their own faith as they try to experience the revelation of the Word of God that is present in the text and appropriate for the context of preaching. However, on every occasion of preaching, the preacher faces the challenge of hearing the good news of the text, of developing a sermon that is inviting to the hearers and then of delivering the sermon in a way that captures and holds the attention of the hearers.

In order to meet these challenges, the preacher maintains communication with God and takes direction from the Holy Spirit, but contextualizing the sermon to fit the occasion of preaching and the congregation to whom it will be preached helps in addressing the issue and even in overcoming the challenge of ensuring that the message of good news reaches the hearers. Ultimately, the work of preaching and the revelation of the Word of God is the work of the Holy Spirit. It is God who initiates the action of revelation. It is God who in self-revelation joins with the spoken words of proclamation, and this occurs in the context of the church, the gathered body of Christ. This is how preaching becomes an act of revelation of the good news of the mitigating grace of God for humanity. Contextualizing the words of the sermon means going beyond the context of the worship experience in which preaching takes place, and where the preacher and the hearers are located, to the wider context of the culture in which the hearers live their everyday lives. In this way, the people experience a new hearing at every event of preaching even when the text is familiar or even well known to the congregation. Contextual preaching allows the congregation to hear, and perhaps even to see, what God has done and is doing in their world. It addresses the reality of the congregation's situation, and in the proclamation of the good news of God's redemptive work the distance of history is overcome, and God is made visible and audible to the people in that time and place.

CONTEXTUALIZATION AS HOMILETICAL CONVERSATION

Within the congregation there are formal and informal groups that share history, are connected by familial ties, have cherished friendships, or are separated by tensions of life and living in community. The conversations within these groupings give substance to the understandings of self, church, community, and the presence of God as active in the many iterations of life. Because these conversations embody and direct how the congregation is constructed, the preacher does well to pay careful attention to them and to the nonverbal interactions of the community. In many instances, the preacher is not an active member of these conversational groups, nor may the preacher be actively or fully aware of the ongoing conversations.

O. Wesley Allen describes the church as a community engaged in ongoing "circles of conversation in which church talk seriously engages all of the other conversations going on in our culture [and] members of the congregation are seen not only as recipients of the church's proclamation but also providers of it."[1] The differing theologies of individuals are often brought to light in the conversational circles that are representative of the beliefs and allegiances of the members of the congregation. The savvy pastor/preacher will be intentional about homing in on these conversations and bringing to light the theologies that are present and operating in the congregation as an initial step to the pastoral task and, by extension, the preaching responsibility. The singular purpose in undertaking this often time-consuming activity is to present the good news appropriately.

Contextualization makes preaching communal, and the conversations of the community are significant for preaching contextually. Through contextualization preacher and people become equal owners of the sermon, and this allows the good news of the sermon to relate equally to both preacher and hearers. The sermon represents ongoing dialogue between three sets of partners—God and the preacher, God and the people, and the preacher and the people. In each case it is true dialogue, a conversation in which the two parties both speak and listen. The preaching event, when it is effective, is representative of the intersection of the three separate yet related conversations.

1. God and the preacher—The preacher's conversation with God through prayer and scripture provides direction for the selection of the good news and the contents of the sermon. Active, daily communication with God enables the preacher to identify the divine voice in the midst of the competing voices of the world.
2. God and the people—God speaks to all people, and in the case of the sermon, God speaks to the hearers to prepare them to receive the Word. The hearers also speak to God asking for a word for their lives, and God is present in the various conversations that take place at the many levels that operate among the people of God.
3. The preacher and the people—This conversation facilitates the preacher's knowledge of what the people expect from the sermon and thus helps to direct the preacher's response to the needs of the

> people. It also helps to verify the accuracy of the preacher's understanding of the conversation with God that determined the contents of the sermon.

The conversations that are part of the communal life of the congregation are essential to the preacher's work of contextualizing the sermon. They also affect the way that we hear and receive the good news of the sermon and help to advance the people of God in their discipleship. These homiletical conversations are essential for the discernment of the gospel message that is offered to address the needs of the people in the particular time and place of each preaching event.

The visiting preacher who cannot be a part of the congregational conversations can nevertheless be part of an ongoing dialogue engaged by the whole people of God. The substance of this conversation is focused on the church and its place and mission in the world. The good news of the presence of God in all of life and in empowering the whole people of God for ministry in the name of Jesus Christ is part and parcel of this dialogue and allows the preacher who does not have access to the specific congregational context to preach in a way that fits the church as the body of Christ.

CONTEXTUALIZING THE GOOD NEWS SERMON

Contextualizing the good news of Jesus Christ in a way that inspires the people as Christian disciples is the ongoing task of the pastor/preacher as a spiritual leader of the church. It is the substance of the church's life and the goal of practical ministry. It is the mission of the church, and it affects the hearers as individuals, the community gathered for the worship of Christ, and ultimately the whole world. When the people receive the good news in a way that touches their lives, they are transformed and they in turn become agents of Christ for the transformation of the world. But whether or not the preacher is also the pastor of the congregation where he or she is preaching, developing and preaching the sermon in a way that makes the good news resonate with the hearers is essential at every moment of preaching.

Contextualizing the good news sermon means shaping the good news in language that is familiar so that the people who hear it can recognize and claim its place in their lives. It means making concrete the Christian message of God's saving grace by applying it directly to the substance of people's everyday lives and offering specific ways in which hearers can be transformed by God's grace to become better disciples of Jesus Christ. It means using language that hearers not only understand but that is meaningful to their lives, that touches them in familiar ways so that they do not need to define the words or interpret their meaning to lay claim to the message. It does not mean being simplistic, but it does mean making the message sufficiently simple that the hearers are not forced to define each word in order for it to make sense to their ears and have influence in their lives.

In addition, contextualizing the good news means recognizing the communal nature of the congregation and allowing the message of good news to impact the corporate life of the church even as it affects each individual personally as disciples of Jesus Christ. Although the preacher preaches one sermon, and each hearer receives the message in the way that makes the offering of good news appropriate to her/his life, true contextualization also considers the community as a body—the body of Christ. The good news of divine love for humanity does not change, and is never exhausted, but placed within the context of the gathered community, it re-forms the people individually and then out of their individualities into one body, under one head, Jesus Christ. In this way the community takes shape and assumes its identity as the body of Christ. Good news preaching keeps present the reality of both the individual and the community under their shared identity in Christ. The good news of the sermon offers the assurance that God is present and at work in the lives of individuals, in the community, and in the world. Contextualizing the good news sermon requires that it be connected not only to the individuals and the gathered community, but also to the mission of Christ in the world. Contextualizing the good news sermon allows the preacher to help the community accept the good news of the gospel as the force for shaping their lives in Christ and for carrying out the mission of Christ in the world.

"TOOLS" FOR CONTEXTUALIZING THE GOOD NEWS SERMON

The tools for preaching exist mainly within the preacher. Although there are methods of creating and preaching the sermon that may be learned, generally the implements required for creating and delivering the sermon lie within the mind and heart of the preacher. Similarly, the tools for contextualizing the good news sermon, when learned, become part of the preacher and part of the natural process of shaping the sermon for presenting good news. The three "tools" necessary for the creation and delivery of contextualized good news sermons are as follows:

> **A theology of good news:** This prepares the preacher to approach the text with expectation and anticipation of finding good news in, behind, beneath, or around the text. A theology of good news gives the assurance that God is always working for the ultimate good of the people of God. It directs the investigation into each text from the position of anticipation of unearthing the evidence of divine grace. It prepares the preacher for the celebration that accompanies the realization of God's active, transforming, empowering presence in human endeavors.
>
> **Knowledge of the context:** Whether pastor or visitor, the preacher must expend the effort that is required to understand the situation of preaching. Knowing the social, cultural, theological, spiritual, and political culture of the people as well as the specific situation of the preaching moment, such as the denominational and liturgical contexts, enables the preacher to develop the sermon in a way that speaks to the reality of the hearers' situation and also to discern corporate needs that can shape the offering of the good news for the congregation.
>
> **The assurance of grace:** The preacher who has an ongoing relationship with God gives witness to the presence of God in the activities of humanity. However, the assurance of divine presence must encompass the belief that God's presence is one of grace.

Frank Thomas expounds on the idea of celebration in preaching, which he says comes from "the assurance of grace."[2] Preaching as part of the liturgy of the church provides a natural place of celebration and a venue for delivering the good news. The preacher must live in the assurance of that God's grace is actively working for the good of humanity in order to develop and deliver good news sermons into the context of the lives of the people of God.

▪ ▪ ▪

Framing the contents of the sermon and the good news appropriately for the congregation is the ongoing task of every preacher. Every sermon is preached into a particular context—of time, place, and people. Even the Word of God whispered into our hearts and minds is contextual. "God's word does not ignore us and our circumstances, speaking imperiously as if none of that mattered."[3] And neither should the preacher. All preaching is contextual, whether or not the preacher designs the sermon with the specific situation in mind. But in order for the good news to reach the hearers in a way that makes it transformative for their lives, it requires full preparedness of self and spirit on the part of the preacher. The preacher prepares to receive good news long before the preparation of the sermon begins, or the moment of preaching is engaged.

THE HOLY SPIRIT IN THE WORK OF CONTEXTUALIZATION

Good news preaching requires that the good news of the sermon is contextualized first for the preacher and through the preacher in the power of the Holy Spirit, for the people. Only in this way can the preacher hope to connect spiritually with the congregation. Even when the preacher has an ecclesiastical relationship with the congregation, it is impossible to bring the good news alive to the congregation, to connect spiritually with the people, unless it is through the power of the Holy Spirit. The Holy Spirit orders the life of the church, and the preacher must tap into that source in order to preach authentic good news to the people of God.

The Holy Spirit is the giver of all gifts that enable the work of the church. The recipients of such gifts are charged in their use "to equip the saints for the work of ministry, for building up the body of Christ" (Ephesians 4:12). In the same way that the preacher's life and ministry is a gift of the Holy Spirit, so too is the specific task of developing the sermon for preaching and for contextualizing the good news of the sermon for the hearers. The preacher who approaches the task without seeking direction from God, and who offers the sermon without the guidance of the Holy Spirit, creates a situation that may result in the message either being rejected or not being heard. However, because the Holy Spirit directs the whole work of the church, the hearers may yet receive good news even in the face of the preacher's omission. Ultimately, good news preaching is effective in its context not simply because of the work of the preacher, but through the preacher by the power of the Holy Spirit. Preacher and people thus experience the good news of divine grace, proclaimed in the words of the sermon and taking effect in the lives of the whole people of God, through the power and presence of the Holy Spirit.

five

Shaping Sermons to Effectively Present Good News

This chapter offers a weekly process for developing a good news sermon. I developed and used this process during my many years as a pastor in a local congregation. I invariably followed the *Revised Common Lectionary* for preaching, and since most of my sermons were expository, the proposed process is directly applicable to that style of sermon. It may be adapted, however, for developing topical sermons, because scripture provides the foundation for all sermons. To that end I have included some suggestions for developing a topical sermon. The process calls for developing the sermon over six days of the week, starting on Monday. If your weekly service of worship occurs on a day other than Sunday, adjust the starting day to the day following the worship service. By spreading the work over six days, you have more time, in the midst of the busy schedule of pastoral duties, to give appropriate attention to the text and to the context of preaching; the material is more likely to be impacted by the context, and you have more time to listen for the internal and external messages that give light and meaning to the text. Further, including your work of developing the sermon as part of your larger weekly schedule within the congregation will allow you to set aside the time you need to prepare well.

If you prefer to prepare your sermons weeks or months in advance, the process can still be used to spread out the activities over a number of days, but be sure to review the sermon two or three days before preaching it to check that it is still contextual for the hearers. The amount of time you have available for sermon preparation depends of course on your schedule, and congregational responsibilities may dictate the days of the week that are most favorable to the work of sermon development, but it is important that the work not be relegated to one day. The process assumes that the preacher reads and studies scripture on a regular basis and is not dependent on the limited time available on a weekly basis to do all the work of interpreting the biblical texts. As interpretive work is done, or as the preacher increases his or her knowledge of scripture and theological understanding, he or she should maintain the material in a way that keeps it available for use in preparing future sermons.

The process assumes also that the preacher has taken or is taking the time to become familiar with the context of the congregation and the preaching event, whether or not the sermon is intended for a regular weekly worship service and the preacher is also the pastor of the congregation. Further, the process assumes that the preacher has daily devotional time that includes prayer and the reading of scripture and perhaps meditation. I suggest that the preacher use part of this devotional time or perhaps extend the length of devotional time on some days for developing the sermon. In any event, throughout the process of sermon development, saturate your work in prayer. The Holy Spirit empowers the preacher in both developing and preaching of the sermon. A schedule that summarizes this process is provided in Appendix D.

This chapter also presents a general outline that may be used for shaping a sermon, describes several common styles of sermon, and shows how to create detailed outlines for several different styles of sermon. The exercise of creating sermon outlines uses the same text to demonstrate how to present the good news garnered from the text and allow it to function as the nucleus around which to develop the good news sermon, regardless of the sermonic style selected for preaching.

A WEEKLY PROCESS FOR SERMON DEVELOPMENT

This process assumes that the preacher, as pastor, is already familiar with the congregation to whom the sermon will be preached, or as a guest preacher has done the work required to be familiar with and understand the preaching context.

MONDAY: READ THE TEXT AND IDENTIFY THE PURPOSE OF THE SERMON

If you have selected a scripture text for preaching, read it as part of your morning devotions and listen prayerfully to the text to hear the specific good news that it offers to the preaching context. If you follow the lectionary for preaching and have not yet selected your text for preaching, read all the scripture passages and listen for the one that resonates spiritually with you, as preacher, and contextually with the situation of the congregation as you understand it. Use lectionary-based devotional material to give you further insights into the text. Read the full pericope and listen carefully for the message of divine grace that arises from the text. Create a Sermon Purpose Statement as a guide to provide focus for your sermon development, including the style of sermon—biblical expository or topical—that you intend to create. If you decide to preach a topical sermon, consider the appropriateness of the topic to the text.

TUESDAY: READ AND EXEGETE THE TEXT

Again, in the interest of time, read the text as part of your morning devotions, but schedule additional time to begin the work of interpretation. If time permits, read more than one translation of the text. The work on this second day of the sermon development process focuses on the interpretation of the text or topic and the identification of the good news and the creation of the discipleship message that will drive the sermon. A helpful exercise for this purpose is described in chapter 2, which identifies the good news and the message to be preached by determining the "what, so what? and so that" of the sermon.

This initial work of interpretation or exegesis involves research and data gathering. In the same way that reading the text brings to the fore ideas that give special meaning to the week's events and conversations, the background data you gather during the research of the text or topic also becomes a lens through which to see and experience the events of the day or the week. As a result, otherwise unimportant actions, tasks, or happenings take on new meaning when observed or experienced through the frame of reference of both the text and its background. These dual filters are helpful in contextualizing the sermon.

This interpretive work of exegesis also requires reflection in order to select what is important to include in the sermon. Good research may unearth significant data that illumines the text; however, such study exegesis is often not appropriate sermon exegesis. I suggest that you make it a practice to access many types of resources for biblical interpretation, including paper and electronic texts and images, and it can be helpful to print out background material if it cannot be easily bookmarked and accessed during sermon writing. Whatever research method you use, and whether or not you use a manuscript for preaching, proper biblical interpretation is a necessity for developing a sermon that offers good news to the hearers.

In every case, whatever the format, the exegesis of the text is necessary for connecting the text with the context and for appropriating the good news of the text for the hearers. Be sure to save any exegetical work that you do, because it is certain that you will use these texts for preaching in the future, especially if you follow the lectionary.

WEDNESDAY: FRAME THE SERMON

In many churches, this midweek day is also the day for adult Bible study led by the pastor, and it can be a difficult day in which to carve out time for sermon development. On the other hand, depending on the schedule of weekly church events, this may be the best day for creating the sermon manuscript. If so, expect to devote a significant part of the day to the task. By this time of the week, you should have most, if not all, of the exegetical work completed and should have a clear idea of the good news you want to share, the message you want to deliver, and the general contents of the sermon, including stories, images, or illustrations you plan to include. Completing the interpretive activities as early as possible in the week allows you time to consider the shape and contents of the sermon. It also leaves you time to shape the sermon in a way that will attract and hold the attention of the hearers.

Whether or not you create a full sermon manuscript, complete any remaining exegetical work today and if you plan to use an outline, develop one based on the style or shape of the sermon you have selected. The outline is the frame within which the substance of the sermon will be housed, and which diagrams the movement that takes the sermon to its planned conclusion. If you choose to create one, the outline of the sermon should be as detailed as is necessary to flesh out the ideas, and as structured as is required to show the flow of the movement of the material being presented to the hearers. Include the intended contents of each part of the sermon and the image or illustrations to be used to give substance to the message. Examples of sermon outlines for several different styles of sermons are included later in this chapter.

In developing an outline, give as careful attention to the introduction and conclusion as you do to shaping the body of the sermon. The more careful and detailed the outline, the easier it will be to review the appropriateness of the contents of the sermon once the manuscript is produced. Often the intended contents or the planned conclusion may dictate a particular sermonic form, or you may select a style of sermon and develop the outline to make the contents fit that shape. In any event you are well served to plan as much of the material to be included in the sermon as possible before actually creating the full-blown manuscript. If you typically preach without a manuscript, this may be the outline you use as pulpit notes when you preach the sermon.

THURSDAY: PREPARE THE SERMON MANUSCRIPT

If you have not done so already, create the sermon manuscript. I highly recommend you create a full manuscript for all sermons. I have heard many preachers who protest the need for a sermon manuscript and profess their ability to preach well without first producing the sermon in written form. While this is true of many gifted preachers, most sermons from preachers who deny the need to prepare a manuscript and claim their ability to preach effectively without such preparation do not live up to the advanced billing. Congregations are not served well by preachers who ramble, lose their place, introduce unnecessary and sometimes erroneous material, leave stories hanging, or otherwise fail at the task of preaching a cohesive, comprehensive, and effective sermon.

Creating a manuscript does not mean you have to preach from the manuscript, but a manuscript does help the preacher to organize the sermonic material in an ordered fashion. It helps to give substance to the ideas that surface in your mind, yet still allows you to review and reshape those ideas for effective presentation. It also helps to ensure that the exegetical material included is appropriate. The Sermon Purpose, Good News and Discipleship Message Statements and the sermon outline already developed help to simplify the task. Once the manuscript is drafted, I recommend that you walk away and allow the material of the sermon to permeate your mind and the heart. If you have done your job well, then the Sermon Purpose Statement, the Good News Statement, the exegetical material, the Discipleship Message Statement, and the sermon outline together will enable you to create a strong sermon manuscript.

FRIDAY: READ, REVIEW, REVISE, REFORMULATE

Read and review your manuscript prayerfully and carefully. Reviewing both text and context. Whether the sermon is biblical expository or topical, and in whatever style it is created, its contents must appropriately connect the biblical foundation with the present situation and needs of the people. In reviewing the manuscript, begin by comparing it against the outline. Is the movement from one section to the next clear and smooth? Do the transitions between sections make sense? If not, prune until they are. Pruning will always help to sharpen your sermon contents, even if it's painful at the time. Review the contents by reading the sermon aloud so that you can experience the sermon through multiple senses—sight, speech, and hearing. Reading the sermon aloud helps you to check the appropriateness of the language, and whether the sermon delivers on its promise of good news and therefore can be heard well.

Learn to listen self-critically to all aspects of your sermon as you read it through. Verify that the contents are appropriate to the shape—for example, the contents of the pages in the Four Pages of the Sermon model, the progression from exegesis to theological exposition to application in the Puritan Plain style, the movement of points to the intended message of good news and the call to Christian discipleship. Verifying the shape helps to ensure that the sermon is designed in a way that facilitates the offering of good news. As for content, review your use of exegetical material, imagery, and illustrations, and verify that the sermon makes sense, that it offers a message that leads to discipleship, and above all, that it clearly offers good news.

Most of the time you will need to make revisions to the draft manuscript—sometimes quite substantial ones, and if the sermon obviously isn't working, have the courage to start over. Once you have made revisions, practice preaching the sermon by reading it aloud, preferably in front of a mirror. This way you actually hear the words or ideas that aren't quite clear or cause you to stumble. If you opt not to preach with a manuscript, be sure you memorize enough of the sermon, and especially the outline and the structure, really well. Resist memorizing the entire sermon, however, as that may make the delivery sound too canned. The sermon would thus lack spontaneity, which might hinder both its reception and the preacher's connection with the congregation.

If instead of a full manuscript, you use an outline or a set of notes, this is also the day to practice using the outline or the notes in practicing to preach a full sermon. Become as familiar as possible with the contents of your sermon. The more prepared you are, the better will be your delivery of the sermon. The more familiar you are with the material of your sermon, the more freedom you have to connect with the congregation when you preach it. The freedom you gain from practicing also gives you more opportunity to experience the presence of the Holy Spirit in your delivery of the sermon.

SATURDAY: REREAD THE SERMON, ABSORB THE MESSAGE, AND RELAX

Whether this is a day of limited parish activity that allows time for relaxation, or if, as in my experience in one parish, it is a day of frenetic activity, try to relax from the work of creating the sermon. You may choose to read the complete sermon as part of the day's devotion or set aside a special time in which to review it. The hope is that by today you are making only minimal changes to the sermon, and you can focus on becoming more familiar with its contents. By this sixth day it is too late to begin writing a sermon or even to make major revisions to a written sermon. Instead of trying to make the sermon a work of perfection, use whatever time you have to become more at ease with your written material.

Other than that, relax! Allow the message to settle deep into your mind and spirit with the assurance that the Holy Spirit will complete the work of preaching by making your sermon take effect in the lives of the hearers.

SUNDAY: PREACH THE SERMON AND LET IT GO!

This is the moment for which you have been preparing throughout the week. If time permits, as part of your personal morning devotion, reread the sermon so that it is fixed clearly in your mind and heart. Resist changing it at this point because that will only confuse you. Trust that you have done what you can and leave the rest up to God—unless of course you notice an egregious mistake, or unless something disastrous has happened in the congregation, in society, or in the world that makes the message of the sermon completely inappropriate. A good example of this is my experience of being called to the bedside of the church organist, who died unexpectedly in my presence very early on the Sunday morning in December that was scheduled as the church's Christmas celebration. Once I arrived at the worship service, I was compelled to change much of both the liturgy and the sermon to allow the church to hear and respond appropriately to the news of the death of a beloved servant of God.

Outside of such extraordinary situations, having been conscientious and faithful to the text and to the process of sermon development, you can rest easy knowing that the good news and the message of discipleship that you have put together in the sermon are appropriate to both text and context. All that is left is for you to trust in divine grace and go forward to offer good news to the people of God. Trust that God will allow the message to reach the hearts of those who need to hear it and relax so that there is also space in your mind and heart for the Holy Spirit to work within you, the preacher.

Although this weekly process has served me well over many years of preaching as pastor in a local congregation, there are many similar models that may work just as well. The important thing is to have a process that is measured and focused over several days. Attempting to do all the work of developing the sermon in one day and at the last minute is foolhardy. More often than not the minimal effort will fail to produce a worthy sermon, and your preaching will be an affront to both the people and to God. As I tell my students, prepare, prepare, prepare! Give the Holy Spirit something to work with!

FRAMING THE OUTLINE OF THE SERMON

Each sermon has three basic and discrete sections:

1. ***Introduction:*** This should capture the attention of the congregation by meeting them where they are, and it should point the direction in which the sermon will move.
2. ***Body:*** This contains the substance of the sermon and makes visible its shape and style. The good news of the sermon is an essential component of this section. This is also the place where the preacher leads out the text biblically, exegetically, and contextually and applies it to the hearers.
3. ***Conclusion:*** This must be concise, and it should provide the opportunity for the hearers to capture the essence of both the good news and the discipleship message of the sermon so that these can take root in the hearts of the hearers and move them to action in the name of Jesus Christ.

The exercise of framing the outline can be a valuable tool for the preacher. Especially when one is caught up in the day-to-day activities of parish life, a brief moment taken to frame a possible outline of an upcoming sermon can go a long way to advancing the process of sermon development. In developing the outline, give as much attention to the contents and structure of the introduction and the conclusion as you do to the body of the sermon.

A good introduction prepares the hearers to receive the message of the sermon. For example, an introduction that makes reference to a familiar event, celebration, or concern may capture their immediate attention. Similarly, ending with a message of good news that is specific to the present lives of the congregation invites the hearers to go forward and do what they heard in the concluding moments of the sermon. A good conclusion encourages the hearers to go forward with the assurance that they can take the action and live out the message of the sermon through the grace of God that was offered in the good news of the sermon.

Whether it is biblical expository or topical, the body of the sermon may be developed in any of several structures or styles.[1] The style of the sermon may be dictated by the scripture text on which it is based, but most often the preacher selects the style that will allow the text to be heard clearly and the message of the sermon to come alive to the hearers. Regardless of the style, the preacher selects the point at which the good news is presented in the sermon. In earlier times, sermons were designed as either deductive or inductive. In the deductive sermon, the preacher begins by laying out the good news, which was then brought to life in the substance of the sermon. The congregation was not required to think through what was being presented in the message as it was clearly spelled out in the sermon. On the other hand, the inductive sermon offered ideas that the hearers were required to analyze so that they would arrive at a conclusion of their own choice. In the inductive sermon, the good news was presented at or close to the end of the sermon. With the inductive manner of presentation, the preacher invites the congregation to join the preacher on the journey that is the sermon and hopefully, arrive at the anticipated outcome of hearing good news along with the preacher. Both biblical expository and topical are genres of sermons within which there are multiple structures or styles. For this writing the material presented for each style of sermon will be based on the selected biblical text. These are by no means the most common or preferred styles; however, they are included to offer a sample selection of sermon structures that may be used for preaching good news to the people of God. The style or structure of the sermon is reflected in the body, which is broken down into discrete sections.

1. Biblical expository sermon that takes a text and engages in biblical interpretation by using any of the types of biblical criticism named earlier, with the intent of determining how the text can speak to the

congregational context, especially as related to the specific purpose the sermon addresses. The interpretation of the sermon includes processes of exegesis, exposition and theological analysis of the text specifically for the purpose of applying the text to the context within which the sermon is preached.

2. Biblical expository using points involves a similar process of biblical interpretation, but in doing so, breaks apart the selected text into defined sections that enable the preacher to connect the text and the congregational context through a series of points that both impart biblical knowledge to the hearers and also relates that knowledge to their lives.
3. Narrative preaching is a style of biblical expository preaching that calls the preacher to retrieve the biblical story and to engage it critically for the purpose of showing its relevance and applying its meaning and importance for Christian living to the present congregation. Narrative sermons enable the preacher to re-tell the biblical story in and through the sermon, bringing alive the presence of God in human endeavors and giving witness to the divine grace that is central to the divine/human relationship.
4. The Journey to Celebration, recognized as traditionally African American, is a form of narrative sermon that also calls forth an emotive response to the biblical text in order to impact core beliefs.
5. The Four Pages of the Sermon interrogates the text to identify human trouble that is offset by divine grace. It connects the trouble and grace in the text with like elements in the world.
6. Topical Preaching focuses the contents of the sermon on a particular topic that is of interest to the preacher and to the congregation. The topic may provide a nucleus for the interpretation of an element of theology, Christian history, Christian doctrine or Christian practice, or may be sparked by a personal or congregational situation, a social concern, national or global issues.

There are many other styles that are directed by the contents of the biblical texts, such as parables that lean toward a narrative or story style or Psalms that favor a verse-by-verse style. Additionally, there are other structures that focus on particular subjects, biblical or otherwise, that are developed to meet pastoral needs in the congregation. It should be noted that the material presented for each style of sermon if applied to a particular congregation, would be modified to fit the congregation, and merely offers a description of elements to be considered in creating the particular style of sermon.

Scripture Text: Mark 10:46–52
[46] They came to Jericho. As he and his disciples and a large crowd
were leaving Jericho, Bartimaeus son of Timaeus, a blind beggar,
was sitting by the roadside. [47] When he heard that it was Jesus of
Nazareth, he began to shout out and say, "Jesus, Son of David,
have mercy on me!" [48] Many sternly ordered him to be quiet, but
he cried out even more loudly, "Son of David, have mercy on me!"
[49] Jesus stood still and said, "Call him here." And they called the
blind man, saying to him, "Take heart; get up, he is calling you."
[50] So throwing off his cloak, he sprang up and came to Jesus.
51 Then Jesus said to him, "What do you want me to do for you?"
The blind man said to him, "My teacher, let me see again." [52] Jesus
said to him, "Go; your faith has made you well." Immediately he
regained his sight and followed him on the way.

- Good News Statement: *Jesus Christ restores us to fullness of life.*
- Discipleship Message Statement: *Christ sees and hears you, so don't give up on your hope for new life.*

SERMON STYLE 1: BIBLICAL EXPOSITORY

This style is simple and is aimed at helping the congregation to have the greatest possible encounter with the biblical text. The exegesis or biblical interpretation of the text locates it in its original context or as close to the origin as possible and offers an exposition of the meaning of the text using both academic information determined by biblical scholars, and material used in the development of sermons by other preachers over time. The interpretation includes theological analysis that deals specifically with the divine/human relationship as seen in the text, specifically what the text says about God, humanity, and the divine/human relationship.

Application of the text brings home the biblical text to the present community in as specific terms as possible. It is the moment in the sermon when the congregation says, "That preacher knows what it is like to be me," and it brings alive to the people the reality of God with us in their situation that may inspire and encourage the hoped-for action of discipleship. The application of the text to the congregational context may also lead the hearers to joy, gratitude, silence, prayer, or other personal or communal response. It is the place where the preacher applies the good news for that unique time and place. In developing the sermon, the preacher may choose to divide the body of the sermon into three distinct sections consisting of exegesis/exposition, theological analysis and application (as shown below), or they may weave together all three elements within the body of the sermon.

Exegesis: Bartimaeus' situation is typical for his time and place. In first-century Palestine, the blind were considered nonpersons in the society, which means that they were prevented from participating in some of the rituals of temple worship even though there were temple laws that provided protections for them. Jesus is on the way to Jerusalem for the last time on the way to the cross, and this is the final healing event before he enters the city.

Theological Analysis: Interpreters suggest that the healing of the blind man is symbolic of the eventual healing of the blindness of the disciples who do not "see" Jesus as the Messiah. Bartimaeus in his physical blindness recognizes Jesus as the Son of David (which means Messiah) and so will the disciples eventually. Further, Jesus' response to Bartimaeus' cry for mercy and healing is also symbolic of Jesus' response to the cries of humanity for healing and restoration from sin. Bartimaeus' healing restores him to a place in the community.

Application: Jesus' response to Bartimaeus' exclusion and specifically the attention given to the man at a time when he is on the way to the cross offers hope for those who feel that life has pushed them to the sidelines and that no one, not even God, has time for them or will listen to their cries for mercy. The story gives them hope and even assurance that Jesus will hear their cries regardless of society's action to the contrary and that through Christ they will be restored to a full place in life and to wholeness of life. By using specific examples of situations that are familiar to the community, the preacher makes the sermon real to the hearers and they connect with the good news of Christ's healing for their own lives and are able to go forward in the spirit of restoration and new life.

SERMON STYLE 2: BIBLICAL EXPOSITORY USING POINTS

Despite the advances in homiletic form and the introduction of many new styles of sermons, many preachers (if not the majority) still preach most sermons in a style that makes points. To be effective, the points should also move the sermon sequentially through the text to the good news. The general rule is three points that may contain subpoints, which in turn provide the substance of the sermon.

Point 1: *Too often we are rejected by society because of our physical appearance.* Bartimaeus was a nonperson in the eyes of his society, as are many in the world, even among the hearers. Sitting by the side of the road, most likely he feels helpless and hopeless about his life. His situation does not permit him to live a full life in his society. This first point not only identifies Bartimaeus' location in time, but it brings into focus the re-identification or non-identification each person may encounter depending on the location in which they find themselves. This first point connects the hearers with Bartimaeus by causing them essentially to sit with Bartimaeus out of the mainstream of life, on the margins of society, because of their identity in the hierarchy of society. There are many examples of current life situations of marginalized persons, perhaps even those in the congregation, that the preacher can use to make the point come alive.

Point 2: *Jesus sees us in the fullness of our humanity as a child of God.* Jesus sees Bartimaeus and each person in the fullness of each one's personhood and reaches past all barriers to provide the life each person needs. The preacher can make the point of Jesus' concern for the marginalized and the invisible among the crowds of life by using Jesus' call to Bartimaeus from the midst of the crowd. The point brings alive the good news that each person has value in the eyes of God, that Christ willingly and readily takes time to hear the cries of the oppressed and the silenced ones. This good news is specific and recognizable. Christ's recognition of the worth of every person at all the times and seasons of life is good news to be shared joyfully and earnestly.

***Point 3:** Jesus gives us hope to face and overcome our life situation.*
Jesus' insistence on having Bartimaeus come to him despite the rejection of the crown offers hope to Bartimaeus and to the congregation. Because Jesus is ready to hear and answer every call, no one need give up hope, even when it seems that life is passing us by. The preacher urges each hearer to remain hopeful in the face of life's difficulties through focusing their faith on Christ. This is a reiteration of the good news, but it is also a charge to the hearers to keep hope alive through the assurance of divine grace. This is the good news that permeates the message and is the main point of the sermon.

SERMON STYLE 3: NARRATIVE

Narrative preaching invites the preacher to re-present the story of God's transforming presence in human endeavors, through a particular biblical story. Narrative sermons enable the preacher to re-tell the biblical story in and through the sermon, bringing alive the presence of God in human endeavors and giving witness to the divine grace that is central to the divine/human relationship. In shaping the narrative sermon, Eugene Lowry's comparison to a novel offers a framework for the step-by-step process. He says the situation of the story "begins with a felt discrepancy or conflict, and then makes its way through complication (things always get worse), makes a decisively sharp turn or reversal, and then moves finally toward resolution, or closure."[2] The challenge for the preacher is not so much in the telling of the story, but in allowing the story to tell the good news of God's presence in the worst that life offers and God's readiness to restore or renew life for and in each person. The sermon outline for the story of Bartimaeus follows the follows Lowry's movements.

Situation: Bartimaeus is a nonperson, invisible to and set aside because of his situation of being blind. Many in the world are relegated to nonperson status and become invisible because of their life situations. We can become nonpersons when we are out of our element or outside our comfort zone, and the feeling is devastating even if it is only for a time. Bartimaeus had no hope of being other than what society had named him, or of having what had been withheld from him, and yet he did not give up hoping.

Complication: Bartimaeus heard about Jesus' passing in his vicinity but had no chance of getting close or being heard because of the crowds. But he held on to hope and shouted for his life. His chance of being seen or heard was complicated by the presence of the crowd and by their demand that he stops shouting out to Jesus. Who or what causes us to stop trying to reach out to Jesus for healing and restoration? Sometimes the crowds are in our own hearts as we doubt that Jesus wants to hear us. This is a common complaint even among Christians, and it may be a place that connects the congregation with Bartimaeus' story.

Reversal: Jesus stops and calls for Bartimaeus. Even in the noise of the crowd, Jesus hears Bartimaeus and does not ignore him; he calls for him. Jesus listens for that lone voice and hears even a faint cry amid all the noises that work to drown it out. This is good news, especially for those who have kept silent for fear of not being heard, or of being heard and ignored or rejected. It speaks to the condition of many within and outside the church.

Resolution: Jesus restores Bartimaeus' sight. Hope is realized and there is great celebration. The message of good news comes alive in the celebration that follows the happy resolution of Bartimaeus' dream of new life. It is a testimony that speaks into the heart of those who still remain quiet, afraid to hope, afraid to call to Jesus, afraid to reach out for fear of rejection. Restoration of life is possible through Christ. Don't give up the hope and don't be afraid to call out; restoration in Christ is still available. The good news of Bartimaeus' restoration engenders hope for personal and communal restoration through Christ. And that is good news.

SERMON STYLE 4: JOURNEY TO CELEBRATION

The idea of a journey that moves to a celebratory conclusion fits as well to frame this story of Bartimaeus' restoration. Frank Thomas describes this process as "Celebration as Ecstatic Reinforcement."[3] This process moves the sermon through three stages, each with a specific emotional process and homiletic intent. The first is situation/complication, which stresses emotive logic with the homiletic goal of getting the people involved and identifying with the story. Cognitive logic is the emotional process that engages the second step of the process, which Thomas names as gospel assurance to complication, in which the good news of scripture serves the purpose of resolving the complication. Once this is done, the homiletic intent is that "emotive logic mandates that the preacher culminates the sermon by ecstatically reinforcing the good news through celebration."[4]

Bartimaeus is on a journey, and it is emotion packed as he strives to rise from his situation, to be heard by the one he believes is the only possible source for his restoration, and to triumph over all odds and regain a place in his society. It resonates with the situation of African Americans who are too often relegated to nonperson status, who are invisible to many, and who are commanded much too often to sit down and shut up. It fits also the intent of the celebratory model in calling the people to a model of Christian living that reaches out to Christ against all odds. The outline for this sermon may be framed as a series of steps—literal steps in the case of Bartimaeus, and figurative and spiritual steps in the case of the congregation. The goal is restoration of life in Jesus Christ. The preacher's focus is helping to direct the people on the journey that leads to the goal of fullness of life, restored through Jesus Christ. At each step the preacher performs a series of tasks that call the people to participate with Bartimaeus on his journey to restoration. Bartimaeus' journey is their journey, and the sermon helps the hearers to feel as Bartimaeus feels so that at the end they can rejoice as Bartimaeus rejoices. Using the stages as defined by Thomas, the journey of the sermon in three steps, each with a series of tasks, is as follows:

Step 1—Situation/complication: This describes Bartimaeus' situation in detailed terms using the exegetical material that brings out the depth of meaning of his position as a blind beggar in that society. The preacher brings the people into the story to sit with Bartimaeus, or even to take on the identity of Bartimaeus. Thomas' emotive logic enables the situations of the text to be applied to the experiences of the people.

- Task A—Bring Bartimaeus' story alive by fleshing out his identity and situation.
- Task B—Set the scene of his placement in readiness for his encounter with Jesus.
- Task C—Connect Bartimaeus with the people by rephrasing his situation in the language of their situation: for example, Bartimaeus sitting by the roadside becomes a single mother sitting in the welfare office with her three small children running around her feet as she feeds a baby. She is a nonperson in the eyes of the people who would be troubled by her presence if they recognized her, so she is ignored.

Step 2—Gospel assurance to complication: Bartimaeus' intent to reach Jesus and be healed is complicated because Jesus is surrounded by the disciples and the crowd, creating a physical distance that is comparable to the cultural distance put in place by the society. The crowd exacerbates the problem by trying to hush Bartimaeus' cries. Move the action along by bringing Jesus, the disciples, and the crowd into the picture.

- Task A—Set the scene by describing the following that Jesus has as he travels. Perhaps compare Jesus to present-day celebrities and the crowds of paparazzi that follow them. Allow Bartimaeus' voice to speak, first without being heard, then with the response of the crowd as being silent.
- Task B—Present Jesus' response to Bartimaeus as the aberration it was, given the norms of the society, and the divine grace it represents. Convert Bartimaeus' voice to the congregation's voice—individually and corporately. Use specific examples that will connect with the actual lives of the people.
- Task C—Apply Jesus' response to Bartimaeus to the lives of the people such that it becomes Jesus' response to each person and to the community. Put Jesus in the community walking through with his entourage and stopping to deal with the addict on the corner, the AIDS patient, the abused mother, the old man on the stoop.

Step 3—Resolution/celebration: The resolution of Bartimaeus' situation comes with the good news (gospel) that Jesus hears him, calls to him, and heals him. This is good news, worthy of celebration, that reaches into the soul of every person who has been ignored or bypassed, whatever the cause. Celebrate Bartimaeus' restoration by naming the promise of restoration to every individual and to the whole community.

- Task A—Remind them that they—each one and the whole community—sit in Bartimaeus' seat, and that they can seek restoration for themselves and for the community by reaching out to Christ in the assurance that Jesus will hear and is ready to respond with affirmation that speaks of restoration.
- Task B—Celebrate Bartimaeus' restoration as that which is promised to each one who calls out to Jesus Christ. Celebrate the assurance that Christ answers the call of each person, hearing the voice, calling forth the person, restoring each in love. As appropriate, call out names of some of those present so that persons become invested in taking the journey to new life. "Call and response" is a common and familiar style of preaching in the African American worship tradition.
- Task C—Repeat the offer of new life and call the community forward to accept the gift. End with the good news that Christ stands waiting in their midst to restore each one to wholeness. The normal ending in African American churches is an altar call, and this may be done using phrasing from the sermon.

The express use of emotion is an important aspect of this model of preaching. Its presence is the expectation of most African American congregations and, when supported by good exegesis and an orderly approach to the goal of a triumphant Christ in the lives of the people, it elicits a deep spiritual response to the good news and to the message of the sermon.

SERMON STYLE 5: FOUR PAGES OF THE SERMON

Paul Scott Wilson's four-page model is both biblical and theological. The biblical facts of trouble and grace in the text are given a theological response that parallels the action of human sin and divine grace in the world.[5] It speaks directly to the good news of God's grace, which triumphs over the trouble caused by human sin. Although pages 1, 2, and 3 may appear in any order, the necessity of presenting page 4 last becomes even more critical for the good news sermon. This model lends itself especially to good news preaching because of the juxtaposition of human sin and divine grace in the sermon.

The action of Bartimaeus' story is almost classic in its presentation of trouble and grace, and the preacher has the somewhat simple task of connecting the situation of the community with the situation of the Bible and the more difficult task of helping the congregation to experience Christ's active presence in their time of need, without making it a sinecure for whatever ails you. The motif of restoration as a consequence of action is an important element in the story that must be brought forward without allowing it to overshadow the free offering of divine grace. The description of the four pages follows, but the subsequent outline used to create a complete sermon will show how they have been used to offer good news in the sermon.

Page 1—Trouble in the Bible: Bartimaeus is on the Jericho Road—a dangerous place. Bartimaeus is blind and a beggar (the two often went hand in hand)—a dangerous life. In fact, Bartimaeus has no real life since he lives outside the community. He is a nonperson who must be silenced when he attempts to speak out and get Jesus' attention.

Page 2—Trouble in the World: Name the many persons in the world whom Bartimaeus represents. Give examples from the community and the larger world society. Provide examples that capture individuals and groups who have become nonpersons in the eyes of their community or the world. Name their need for restoration to fullness of life.

Page 3—God's Grace in the Bible: Jesus hears Bartimaeus, stops, and calls for him. Jesus connects with him by speaking directly to him and asking about his need. Jesus heals him and restores him to community. Jesus' action is not simply about healing; by speaking directly to Bartimaeus he also recognizes and honors his identity. Jesus' action is in response to Bartimaeus' need.

Page 4—God's Grace in the World: Jesus hears and has heard the calls from each person. Jesus speaks—is ready to speak—directly to each one. Jesus responds—is ready to respond—to each person's need. Jesus offers restoration of life to each person—the good news. The substance of restoration is in response to the need, and it is individual. Jesus restores each one to fullness of life. God's grace is always good news, and the promise of restoration is the good news that the biblical story portrays, and that the preacher may use to bring light to the restorative grace of God that is available to all people.

SERMON STYLE 6: TOPICAL SERMON

In topical preaching, the topic is the focus around which the contents of the sermon center. A preacher may choose a topical sermon when the focus transcends a single biblical text or theme; when specific, significant and appropriate theological interpretation is required, especially in the face of what seems like a challenging or necessary biblical mandate. The selected topic may represent focused teaching on a particular biblical, theological, social, or other issue that is deemed important to the life and health of the congregation. Although the topic is usually selected first, a topic may arise from a biblical text. Generally, the sermon is divided into points that enable the preacher to interpret the topic from scripture to the congregation. Applying the topic of "Hope in Christ" to the story of Bartimaeus, the outline of the sermon may be as follows:

Point 1: Too often, because of our life situation, it is difficult to have hope. Bartimaeus' situation at the side of the road away from society made it difficult for him to hope for a better life. When we are consistently marginalized by society, it is difficult for us to believe in or to have hope for our lives.

Point 2: When an opportunity comes our way, our hope in Christ enables us to move beyond the situation in which we find ourselves. Despite his blindness and his location at the side of the road, on hearing of Jesus' presence, it was hope in Christ, even if only a remnant, that enabled Bartimaeus to cry out persistently to get Jesus' attention.

Point 3: Christ's promise of new life fills us with hope. When Jesus called to Bartimaeus, his hope was not only renewed. It was fulfilled by the restoration of his sight, which also restored him to society. The congregation can be encouraged to hold on to hope for a better life by trusting in the presence of God with them at all times.

Regardless of the style of the sermon, whether biblical expository or topical, and whatever the structure, the recognition of the biblical text as foundational to the sermon means that exegesis or interpretation of the text is essential to developing every sermon. The application of the text to the people's situation, the context in which the sermon is to be preached, gives life and meaning to the sermon. Without such application, the sermon is void insofar as it hopes to offer good news to the hearers. The good news is ever and always divine love that offers life and hope and joy and peace to all people.

six

Delivering the Sermon as a Good News Message

Although I have several books of sermons, have studied large numbers of written sermons, and even wrote my dissertation on the sermons of John Wesley, I find it difficult to get enthusiastic about reading sermons. Generally, my mind wanders trying to imagine how the preacher told the story, or expressed the urgency of the material, or encouraged participation of the congregation in the proclamation of the word. Preaching is a spoken art, and the road between text and proclamation, between developing and preaching the sermon, is long and tricky and littered with many ideas, practices, and methods of presentation that did not work.

In my classes I stress the importance of pulpit presence, and students are evaluated on the presentation and delivery of their sermons almost as much as they are on the structure and content of each sermon. The ideas in this book are ones that I have used in my seminary classes, but without being actually present with you to demonstrate what I am hoping to teach, it becomes difficult to put them into words and troublesome to imagine that someone might be misled or misdirected as that person reads into or out of the ideas in this chapter erroneous or contrary advice. This chapter addresses parts of the preaching task that affect both the delivery and the receipt of the sermonic message: the language of the sermon, the location of preaching, embodiment by the preacher, and ways of overcoming distractions to ensure that what is delivered by the preacher is indeed good news.

LANGUAGE

Language, like preaching, is always contextual, and the preacher's language combined with the language of the sermon (they are not necessarily the same) must resonate with the language of the hearers if they are to hear a message of good news from the mouth of the preacher. In addition, the preacher's imagination—a gift of God—in tandem with the work of the Holy Spirit, helps to make sermons listenable. On many occasions I have heard sermons that have been delivered in a tone and pitch that have convinced many that they represent the work of the Holy Spirit but that not only contained no good news but were also weak in content and shaky in structure. On the other hand, I have heard many sermons that have been erudite and well-structured but that have been delivered in such a joyless, unenthusiastic manner that the congregation—those who were not asleep—simply ignored the preacher as they gazed out with unfocused eyes. Obviously, we need balance; and as a contextual art, preaching that is effective in one culture or congregation is not necessarily effective in another.

In the foreword to Ronald Sleeth's text *God's Word and Our Words*, Thomas Long writes, "because God's Word finds expression in human speech, it can never be confined to the cultus but moves to embrace the world. It can never be frozen and codified into a set of principles or eternal verities but remains alive, active, dynamic."[1] In short, words matter. Words are a dynamic expression of the culture, ever changing, ever being created, ever reframed in their use. Keeping abreast of the descriptive words that speak to a culture is essential to preachers because words change with the passing of each day.

In the movie *Akeelah and the Bee*, a story about words, Akeelah is challenged by her coach about the use of a slang word. Her response is to open the latest version of the dictionary and respond with the recorded definition of said word. She reminds her teacher (and every preacher who understands and appreciates the value of words in the sermon) that language is a living art. To put a slightly different slant on Ronald Sleeth's words, "it should be good news that the words [original Word] they preach [are] alive and dynamic and . . . can be a means of grace."[2] I make the change unapologetically because I believe that what we preach is the Word of God only as the Holy Spirit transforms the words that we speak.

The language of the sermon must not only be contextually dynamic, it must be easily understood. The congregation, even when it consists of biblical scholars, does not have the time, and certainly not the inclination, to translate the language of the sermon into ordinary language. The sermon is not an academic paper and, although we worship God with heart and mind, the sermon is (or must be) aimed at the heart if it is going to affect the hearers spiritually for their Christian discipleship. The caveat to this directive is the problem of talking down to the community. While the hearers of the sermon may be the children of God, they are not all children in age, and they deserve the respect of the preacher who, though seminary trained and even scholarly, is on equal footing in the eyes of God, whose Word we are all called to preach. The language of the seminary is not the language of the church in its identity as the gathered community. The words of the classroom or the scholar do not necessarily represent the language of the people in the pews. Seminary teaches us important theological words, and while, as Lucy Lind Hogan tells us, "our listeners are certainly able to learn what they mean, it can be frustrating when a preacher sprinkles the sermon with 'theologese,' either forgetting that others do not speak that language or trying to impress the listeners with how learned he or she is."[3] Indeed, we are charged to use words that resonate with the people in their location, whatever that may be.

CONVERSATIONAL LANGUAGE

Preaching is not merely dialogical (that is, between two persons), it is (or should be) conversational. The preacher engages in a three-way conversation with God and the people of God. And, in fact, since there is truly no single corporate voice in the church, the conversation partners have the ability to multiply exponentially as more hearers/speakers enter the realm of the conversation engaged by the preacher through the sermon. Lucy Rose offers a conversational mode of preaching in which, "by realizing that although one may do the speaking, the preacher is never isolated or alone."[4] The conversational sermon invites the hearers to reflect and respond not simply to the preacher but to the words as well. Wes Allen, following Rose's lead, notes that in conversational preaching, "preachers, out of the depths of their convictions and experiences, propose a tentative interpretation of scripture and of the life of the congregation for the additions, corrections, and counter proposals."[5] This sounds suspiciously like the talk-back format of the African American church! Where the African American church's talk to the preacher is in support of that very kerygmatic expression named by Rose, a conversational approach invites substantive dialogue with the preacher of the Word of God.

What does this do for the good news aspect of the sermon? If the preacher is the one speaking on behalf of the many, and especially on behalf of God, then the preacher's conversation, the sermon, must be representative of the covenantal connection that is divine grace, which is the requirement and center of every sermon. Good news preaching cannot thus be other than conversational since the divine/human relationship that the preacher expounds is not limited to the preacher. The whispers of God that nudge us to proclaim the good news of divine grace are not directed only to the ears, heart, or mind of the preacher. God's Word comes to every person, "meets our condition, emerging quietly and most often unnoticeably in the midst of who and where we are."[6] And when it comes, perceived or not, it requires engagement by the preacher to become the proclaimed Word that invites celebration of the good news of God's redeeming grace for all people.

INCLUSIVE LANGUAGE

Although the use of inclusive language in writing and in public speaking is required at my seminary, the majority of students who enter my second-year class preach with a mouthful of exclusive words. Both women and men of the church still find it difficult to speak inclusively about the divine. Some mistakenly (in my opinion) change to a feminine pronoun for God in the hope that it will be taken as a sign of their inclusivity of speech. And while I understand the intent and appreciate how unwieldy the words of the sermon can become when one tries to avoid the use of pronouns—whether masculine or feminine—when referring to God, there is seldom a time when I do not call the student to account for the misuse of language.

The good news of divine grace is that it is open and available to all. It is God's precious gift to the people of God—not gender selective, and not color blind. God in divine wisdom made us in different genders, in all colors of the earth, for God's glory. In God's mind there is no barrier of language or origin that separates us from God. The good news is for all equally, and each individually. Those who still balk at the requirement and who use non-inclusive language for God or for human beings are, wittingly or not, supporting separation or discrimination that is not good news. Exclusive language for God and people makes of the church a hierarchical, unjust entity. Unfortunately, that way of identifying God remains in use in many places and by many people, some happily and unapologetically. But, despite claims to the contrary, there cannot be good news in such places. The source of divine grace is also the seat of justice, and exclusivity among the people of God speaks of injustice that is contrary to the love of God.

Inclusive language is also liberative. To be inclusive is to remove all barriers that might hold some people back from receiving the benefits of being part of the body of Christ. At the same time, it frees some who would withhold access to the good news from those who need to hear it. So, it is not only liberative, but also emancipatory. It is open and inviting, making room for all to speak and all to be heard. It is understood through the heart and not simply the mind. As such it speaks beyond the natural differences that exist because of the global locations. The language of good news is inclusive in all aspects of human understanding, offering joy and peace, hope and love, and grace upon grace that comes through the presence of the Holy Spirit, who orders our speech in the name of the divine.

The language of the church, the language of the preacher, and the language of good news preaching when representative of the love of God, is undeniably inclusive. The preacher is commissioned to lead the church, and to engage the hearers in the open conversation initiated or continued by the sermon. If God is a welcome part of that conversation—and God must be if it is to have substance for the life of the people of God—then the name of God and the name of all the people of God must be said without equivocation or the segregation that non-inclusive language supports and promotes. Preaching is an act of the church, and good news preaching is located only in the church that acknowledges and lives into the reality of unfettered grace. Paul asked, "What are we to say? Should we continue in sin in order that grace may abound? By no means!" (Romans 5:1). Can the church or the preacher continue to exclude the people of God because of language? By no means. Good news preaching requires language that is grace-full and meets the context of the beloved community, those who represent the inclusive body of Christ.

LOCATION

Preaching is a liturgical act that takes place in the midst of the gathered community. The impact of the location on the efficacy of the sermon is an essential ingredient for preaching good news. As preachers, we must consider the location in which the sermon will be preached in order to accommodate the fit between the sermon, the style of presentation, and the response of the hearers. The ultimate purpose of this chapter is to impress upon preachers the importance of good delivery in good news preaching. Good news preaching requires both development and delivery that take seriously the understanding of preaching as the act of proclaiming the gospel of divine grace.

Preaching is an act of the church. For the most part, preaching occurs in the context of church worship services and is a prominent part of the service. "What might our sermons be if preachers seriously acknowledged the Church?"[7] This important question framed by Richard Lischer calls preachers to understand more clearly their responsibility to the life of the church—that is, to more clearly offer good news that can make a difference in individual lives and in the life of the gathered community.

We explored the contextualization of the sermon in chapter 2, within the subject of exegeting the congregation. Recognizing that God breaks into our history and the history of the church, and being fully aware of our past, present, and the ever (and more quickly) changing future, we believe that "God who works incarnationally, weaves the past together in fresh and redemptive ways moment by moment."[8] That means that there is always good news, and the church is the place of proclamation of the good news. This is why not only do our sermons address the reality of the congregation's situation, but why, at every event of preaching, we preachers are called to offer the grace of God new again to the people. When we do this, we reveal once again who God is for us in the present. That is good news preaching!

THE LOCATION OF WORSHIP

Worship reveals God. Preaching proclaims the Word of God, and through that proclamation God is revealed. Thus, preaching and worship stand together. Preaching occurs in the context and location of worship, and preaching is an act of worship. Charles Rice suggests that the connection between preaching and the gathered community may be strengthened liturgically in part because "more attention to liturgy might well change the way we preach."[9] Liturgy is the work of the people; it is worship of God offered in community. And the preaching of the church takes place in the community of the people of God gathered for worship. The preacher stands in the action of remembering that binds the community. Through the words of the sermon, the preacher invites the people to participate actively in remembering God's grace, receiving that grace for themselves, and participating in the work of grace in the world. Preaching that is located in the context of worship has corporate ownership and responsibility. It is the people's representation of the Word of God alive in a place where God reveals God's self.

Worship as God's self-revelation and the people's response calls forth an equal response from the preacher as from the people. This is why the worship centers of initiating and sustaining grace—the baptismal font and the communion table—are best located in full view of the place of proclamation lest the preacher lose sight of his or her own need for the same grace that is offered in the sermon. As Rice notes, "the preacher stands in the same place where every Christian is placed and formed . . . and it is this same reality that forms the preacher and that tests each sermon."[10] Good news preaching offers a reminder to the gathered community—including the preacher—that every person stands in need of covenantal grace, and that each is a recipient of divine grace. The proclamation of the good news serves as a reminder to the whole people of God that grace abounds. It is good news preached to, by, and for the whole people of God. It is the liturgy of the church, located in the context of the worship life of the church.

THE GATHERED COMMUNITY AS THE LOCATION

Preaching is a symbol of the church. That means that preaching is connected first and foremost with the church—the gathered community under the lordship of Jesus Christ. Preachers are generally expected to engage the art of preaching within a church building or a worship service that is connected with the church. Like other symbols of the Christian faith, such as the sacraments, preaching is symbolic of the mission and ministry of the church of Jesus Christ. The church exists wherever and whenever the people of God gather to celebrate the presence of God in their individual and corporate lives. The people in their gathering constitute the body of Christ, a microcosm of the beloved community formed and gathered under the lordship of Jesus Christ. Preaching the Word of God occurs in the gathering of the people, and as such it is symbolic of the active, enduring presence of God.

As a symbol of the church, good news preaching reminds the people of God's creative, redemptive, and transformative presence. Good news preaching testifies to the enduring grace of God that is at the heart of the interaction of God and humanity. Good news preaching symbolizes the presence of God revealed through the words of the sermon, which, through preaching, become the Word of God. Through the preached word, the people are invited into communion with God, and although it is not a sacrament as experienced through Holy Communion, the preached word nevertheless brings the people into communion with Christ, the head of the church.

EMBODIMENT OF THE SERMON

Embodiment refers to the way in which the preacher uses his or her body to impart the message of good news. Regardless of one's physical state, the preacher must work to prevent that physical state from distracting hearers from receiving the message. The preacher's presence is a critical ingredient in making the sermon truly a message of good news. The story is told of the preacher who wagered that in the same sermon he could cause half the congregation to weep copiously and the other half to laugh hysterically. He won the wager by attaching a tail to the back of his pants, and as he preached a stirring, highly emotive sermon to the congregation facing one side of the church, his tail bobbed up and down, causing raucous laughter from those on the other side. Suffice it to say that his was not a faithful embodiment of the sermon.

Preaching and listening to sermons are both multisensory activities, and while the preacher's task is directed to inducing a particular emotion in the listening congregation, the congregation is affected by the way in which the preacher embodies the sermon. The delivery of the good news sermon is as important as its creation. The preacher therefore does well to be attentive to the need to engage the hearer to see, hear, touch, taste, and even smell the grace of God. The senses with which God gifted us are so important in experiencing God's gift of life that when one sense is lost, another tries to compensate for the lost sense. It is commonly believed that persons who have lost their sight have sharper hearing. Whatever the truth of that statement, the savvy preacher considers the different ways in which people receive information and the importance of preaching to all the senses of the hearers. Such preachers also pay attention to the issues of life that may overshadow or mute the words of the sermon and are intentional about finding ways to ensure that every effort is made to ensure that all persons who are present in one way or another can receive the message in one form or another.

The movement of the whole body gives substance to the embodiment of the message of good news. For example, the voice utters the words that become Word; the eyes, windows of the soul, reveal the preacher's inner conviction of God's love and the commitment to sharing with and inviting others into that love; the gestures give expression of both invitation and conviction; and the body's movement demonstrates the energy of God's sustaining power that gives strength to the work of proclamation. Our body language sends a message along with or in contradiction to the words we speak. The preacher who, in offering good news in the sermon, looks and acts in a way that demonstrates that he or she is also the recipient of the good news will present a more believable sermon to the hearers. Divine grace is good news worth shouting from the housetops! The preacher who comes dragging into the pulpit and reads from a manuscript with little or no expression and even less energy cannot hope to deliver any kind of good news to the congregation, regardless of what is written in the sermon or how well the good news message is expressed. Since the demeanor of the preacher lacks credibility, the people cannot hear the words.

The embodiment of the sermon speaks in part to the preacher's knowledge of the words of the sermon, but it speaks even more clearly to the preacher's own faith in and acceptance of the message of grace that the sermon offers. During their practice preaching, many students become self-conscious about their bodies and are sometimes excessively concerned about their pulpit presence. Yet many of those same students resist the idea that preachers could or should practice their delivery, and they express unnecessary discomfort through the entire sermon. In some cases, students are stricken by vocal mannerisms that are so distracting that they become the listeners' focus. As human beings we are connected in mind, body, and spirit, and all three elements of our being must be engaged in preaching. The good news of the sermon is a gift of divine grace, and we preach it best when we are the embodiment of the good news of God's grace for all people.

DELIVERING THE GOOD NEWS

The heart of the matter when it comes to preaching rests on the effective delivery of the good news. Any distraction to the preaching of the sermon, whether it is the way we use our voice, hands, eyes, or any other part of the physical body, can obstruct the hearing of the good news. Distractions cause the words of the sermon to take second place in the act of preaching, and the message to the hearers is filtered through the distractions, and the good news cannot be heard clearly. Some hearers may still receive the good news and may still hear the call to discipleship, but undoubtedly some will be unable to focus because of the distractions, and still others may abandon the effort to try to discern good news. The preacher is called to attend to sermon delivery and body language to the same extent that they attended to developing the contents of the sermon. Since the original publication of this work, the world has suffered through a global pandemic. Mandatory lockdowns forced the church to re-group in order to continue its delivery of the preached message. Preachers were required to find new and different ways of preaching, of delivering a message that would reach the people despite the reality of being apart from one another.

The pandemic caused immeasurable loss. However, it also brought unexpected but welcome developments in methods of preaching to non-existent, distant, unheard, and even unseen congregations. Where before the preacher's attire contributed to the presentation of good news preaching, no longer did the preacher's attire work to support or deny the grace of God resident in the life and work of the preacher. And the issue of whether one donned cassocks, robes, suits, dresses, clergy collars, or any other style clerical of dress became almost moot as the attention of most preachers was centered on caring for their congregations at a distance.

However, pastors still needed to prepare and deliver sermons. In some cases, the challenge intensified as preachers found their sermons visible or available to persons with whom they had no relationship, but who, perhaps more than ever, needed to hear good news. Since the subject of this section is embodiment of the good news sermon, the issue of many preachers not knowing what to do with their hands, or how to stand or sit, what facial expressions were appropriate, and how to modulate their voice when the sermon is preached into the air, still required preachers to be aware of possible distractions to the message. For some, good or appropriate gestures do not come naturally or easily. My advice to practice preaching the sermon in front of a mirror has met resistance by some preachers who say that does not work, as it makes them look stiff. But I stand by the belief that good presentation most often comes with good knowledge of the sermon and the conviction that its message is true. So even though practicing before a mirror might not work perfectly, it helps the preacher become familiar with the text, so that in the actual event of preaching, they can be freer to use different aspects of the body, apart from the voice, to deliver the good news message. The preacher who knows the material is free to concentrate on sharing the message of the sermon with the congregation and finds there is little or no need to be concerned with his or her hands. In fact, the hands take on a life of their own as they also participate in getting the message of good news across to the people. I consider this the work of the Holy Spirit and that holds true with every congregation, even those that the preacher cannot see.

One preaches with the whole body. Paying attention to extraneous utterances (for example, uh, ah, um) and movements or mannerisms such as clearing the throat often, repeatedly touching the ears or nose, or pushing back hair or spectacles, can prevent such distractions from overshadowing the content and especially the good news of the sermon. Good news preaching calls the preacher to embody the sermon joyfully, to make eye contact with the people to whom the message is directed, to show belief and excitement about the good news. Being familiar with the contents enables the preacher to be less bound to the sermon manuscript or notes, whether on a computer, notebook, phone, or paper. The medium itself does not matter to most people, but the handling or the dependence on it to the exclusion of the people reduces their ability to hear and receive the good news. The use of videos is almost taken for granted and congregations, having returned to their sanctuaries, have become accustomed to using media in connection with preaching. What is still of primary importance in preaching is that the preacher takes all the steps necessary in both the development and the delivery of the sermon to ensure that the gospel comes alive to the people and that the good news of God's grace is seen and heard and ultimately lived by preacher and people—the whole people of God.

CONCLUSION

I believe that every preacher is responsible for offering the good news of divine grace every time he or she preaches. That grace is the only hope that anyone has of overcoming sin, and preachers who have accepted the task of proclaiming that good news do so by the very grace of God he or she preaches. As preachers we speak of divine justice and mercy, and through the words of the sermon we offer both a warning against sin and death, and an invitation to life, both present and future, through God's redeeming grace. Preparing a sermon often resembles a balancing act as the preacher strives to offer realistic and visible good news of God's transformative grace without bypassing the critical and similarly responsible act of alerting the hearers to the sin that is present and visible in human life. Good news preaching keeps in focus the saving, enlivening presence of God that justifies and sanctifies repentant humanity. While the sermon as a medium of presenting this good news and the preacher as the proclamatory voice are critical ingredients in sharing the good news with the people, it is the Holy Spirit who gives life to the content of good news for both preacher and hearers.

When we accept scripture as the inspired Word of God and give careful attention to biblical interpretation, we can connect the written contents of scripture with the content of the lives of the hearers. Many preachers successfully motivate their hearers to live better lives, but only scripture provides proof positive of God's concern for and engagement with the lives of ordinary people in a way that has stood the test of time. Applying scriptural truths to human life through God's grace is what motivates and sustains hearers throughout their lives.

The good news preacher willingly delves into all of scripture to unearth the enlivening, sustaining presence of God in the past, connects it with the present lives of the people, and presents it as both current reality and future promise and hope. But the words become Word for both preacher and hearers only through the transforming presence of the Holy Spirit. In ongoing conversation with the people, the preacher may discern the effectiveness of his or her preaching. Appendix E offers a simple form that may be used to receive immediate feedback on preached sermons.

Hearers can tell when the preacher understands their situation in part by the way in which the preacher presents God's grace in the sermon. Divine grace is good news for everyone, but the application of God's grace to the situation of preaching gives the assurance that God's presence in the midst of the people relates directly to their needs and their hopes. Even in the face of the world's sin and degradation, the good news preacher keeps hope alive by preaching the good news of divine grace.

As preachers we experience the presence of the Holy Spirit in prayer and through our witness to God's grace, and this gives credence to the words of our sermons. At the heart of the sermon is the grace of God. The good news of the sermon is not merely the interpretation of a scripture text or topic brought to life through in-depth study, or even particularly the preacher's internalization of the Word and connection with the hearers. And although we may preach the good news that we have experienced in our relationship with God, the good news of our sermons is not about us. It is about God's grace present and available to all people for all time. And when we offer it to the people of God in our sermons—that's good news preaching.

four
Good News Sermons

A DIFFICULT REQUEST

This sermon was preached at a Chapel service during Black History Month at Garrett-Evangelical Theological Seminary.

SCRIPTURE TEXT: 2 Kings 2:1–12

SERMON STYLE: Biblical Expository

SERMON PURPOSE STATEMENT: In view of the ongoing challenge about making right decisions experienced by the students regarding their call to ministry, I want them to experience the assurance of God's anointing grace guiding and empowering them to carry out their ministry, by means of a biblical expository sermon based on the story of Elijah and Elisha and the passing of the mantel.

GOOD NEWS STATEMENT: God anoints us for service in answer to God's call on our lives.

DISCIPLESHIP MESSAGE STATEMENT: Stay focused, and experience the transforming, transfiguring grace of God.

Recently one of my young sister colleagues in ministry called me to request my help in dealing with a pastoral situation. The powers that be had decided, as part of a wider strategy for the churches in her area, to close the two churches under her charge, get rid of one building completely and use the other building for some new and unnamed or even undetermined mission venture. There would be no more Sunday worship services in either of the two locations, and the people would be free to attend any of the two remaining congregations in her area that would continue to exist virtually unchanged.

What she was being asked to do was to prepare the people to accept the decision that had been made without any warning or consultation of either the pastors or the congregations that were being affected. Talk about a difficult request, she was angry on her own behalf and on account of the people to whom she had been providing pastoral leadership for the past two and a half years. Then in the midst of that, she was presented with a new appointment to a vibrant, active, engaging congregation. For her, delighting in what was about to come in her own new pastoral opportunity was almost an impossibility, as she tried to deal with her own grief and that of her congregation. Any change has some element of difficulty, and the changes that come our way in life, whether they are expected, anticipated, or seemingly out of nowhere, may challenge us. But I believe the most difficult change to deal with is when it represents the movement of God in our lives.

That is the situation that confronts Elisha. Happily plowing his parents' fields, Elisha has been approached by Elijah and without any warning has been called into service by the prophet of God. After his encounter with God following his meltdown, Elijah had been instructed to anoint Elisha as his successor, and he promptly sought out this young man, throwing his cloak over him as the mark of succession. And Elisha, understanding this unspoken message, this divine command, had simply ceased his task and followed his new teacher. Scripture does not tell us, but Elisha's readiness to follow Elijah leads us to believe that Elisha welcomed this new life opportunity. And we don't hear anything more of Elisha until this moment when it is time for him to assume the responsibility for which he has been preparing; to make the really big change that moves him way beyond his comfort zone.

Let me pause a moment and ask what may be a difficult question for some of you to answer. Can you remember the moment when you felt the mantle of God's call drop on you? Was there a moment when you knew in your heart that this calling for which you are being prepared was made real in your heart? When did you know; how did you know that coming here, being here was what you were meant to do? There are many persons who come to seminary with only a vague idea about the rigorous preparation it takes to earn a Master of Divinity degree in order to take on some type of pastoral leadership is what they are being called to do. But like I was, they are commandeered to engage the rigor of seminary education. And they do it because there seems to be no choice—that's my story and I'm sticking with it.

As I said a little while ago, we are not told exactly what Elisha is given to do in order to prepare for this moment of transition. We don't know specifically what the liminal space of his seminary education looked like. But if you follow Elijah's trajectory after he took on Elisha as his student, especially his dealing with Ahab, it should give you an idea that Elisha did not have an easy time of it getting accustomed to the rigor of the prophetic role that awaited him. It should give you pause as you enter those arenas of study and preparation for ministry called seminary classes, with the idea that it should be a walk-over that requires very little effort and that should result automatically in the highest possible grade. Preparing to do the work of God faithfully and effectively is a hard thing, a difficult decision—make no bones about it.

The journey to the place of transfiguration of both Elijah and Elisha was a hard one for this young prophet. But it was also hard for his teacher. I'm sure Elijah had carried out the divine command to prepare his student as faithfully as he possibly could. Most likely he had kept him by his side when he had to deal with Ahab's greed and willfulness over the taking of Naboth's vineyard. Can you imagine how Elisha must have trembled when his teacher had to confront and condemn the king over his actions. He must have wondered in his heart whether he could be so bold, even with God at his side. And dealing with Jezebel, who had such great influence over her husband Ahab, and the whole issue of the worship of Baal, what a trial that must have been. Remember Elijah had to deal with all the kings following Ahab's death, with the people's continued fascination with other gods; their continued defiance of the first commandment as they again and again put the gods of Baal before the true and living God of their ancestors; and above all, with the challenge as the prophet of God to bring a message to Israel that spoke of their doom. What kind of job is that? Why should anyone be anxious to take on that challenge? Indeed, it's a difficult decision to be called to make.

Many years ago, at another seminary, I had the a student, who preached a very stirring sermon in class, in which he asserted that Elisha did not want to heed the request of his teacher, a request made three times in the passage that you heard read from 2 Kings 2, to wait at specific points along the journey from Gilgal to the Jordan, because he was lazy. Well, I don't think that was Elisha's problem, nor do I think this story of leadership transference is one of unwillingness or even inability or insecurity with respect to the work of being the mouthpiece of God to which every prophet is called. There are many themes that come out of this story, but for this little while let's look at it from the perspective of commitment or said more theologically, covenant. There is a whole lot of covenant-keeping visible in this text and it involves not only the humans, but unsurprisingly, we see God's faithfulness in keeping covenant with the people of God.

Let's look at Elijah for a moment. Elijah has faithfully discharged his mission as the prophet of God, speaking truth to power again and again and when God told him get ready to see the end of your task and prepare your successor, he didn't blink. He went at God's command and took Elisha under his wing, teaching him and preparing him to do the work of God. For many, if not all of us, the role of teacher that we are called to wear is one that represents a commitment to covenant-keeping. Our mission is not simply to get our students ready for doing the work of God, but it is our ministry, our side of the covenant that we have made with God. And in keeping that covenant, we cannot let our students avoid or not take seriously the rigor of being faithful to the covenant they have made. God's promise to Elijah, which will be realized fully in Elijah's transfiguration and his ascension into heaven did not come because he shirked or skated by his task. Covenant-keeping for Elijah meant doing the hard things, speaking out even when it made him unpopular with kings and with people—even his colleagues, the band of prophets. And in this moment of transition, a moment that brings about his transformation from the physical to the spiritual, even in this moment of great glory, he does not shirk on that final work that God had given him. He has one eye on the culmination of his journey and another on his spiritual child.

Elijah knows how difficult it will be for his spiritual son to witness his departure. He wants to spare Elisha the pain of loss that comes with any transition, and he urges Elisha to stay behind, in order that he would not have to deal with the pain that comes with the loss of a loved one—no matter to what end. Mark with me the places where Elijah urges Elisha to wait, and their significance for the people of Israel. Gilgal, Bethel and Jericho were representations of God's covenantal promise fulfilled to the people. And Elijah urges his mentee into a time of reflection that will allow him to ponder not only the task that is ahead but to reflect on his own place and the necessity for his own covenantal commitment as a prophet of God. Along the journey to the place where God is leading us, there are for each of us stopping points along the way. Each of us is called to decide whether we will take time to reflect on what God is calling us to do, whether we will take seriously the covenant that our ministry represents, whether we are prepared for the difficulties that await us as we resolve to do the work of God faithfully.

Given that this is Black History Month, I would be remiss if I did not mention our ancestors in the struggle, who refused to be stopped along the way to the place of God's determination; who knew that what lay ahead was perhaps pain and death, loss and grief; but kept their faces steadfastly fixed on the God who they knew walked beside them to the freedom that God had already given them as part of the divine covenant. Those men and women, young and old made perhaps the most difficult decision of their lives thus far; walked the difficult journey involved in escaping the degradation of slavery, refusing to turn back no matter how many times the prophets of their days, many of whom had already earned the title of false prophets, told them to turn back.

Elisha would not turn back. Instead, he asked his teacher to name him once and for all the favored Son. But Elijah could not. He responds to Elisha: "You have asked a hard thing." Or as the Common English Version puts it, "You have made a difficult request." It's hard and difficult because the gift or the anointing of the Spirit of God comes only from God, and it is given only at God's behest. Elisha wants a double portion according to the custom of the culture for a first son to receive, but what Elijah tells him is that he will have to depend on God for that gift. And it is perseverance, determination, covenantal commitment, that enables us to receive the gift that is ours by divine grace.

Along the journey of his prophetic life, God had been with Elijah. He had shown up in awesome power, as a force to be reckoned with against the prophets of Baal that Elijah killed by the hundreds, or in a still small voice, when Elijah suffered a major meltdown when fleeing for his life after that great showdown. But more than that, all along the journeys of God's people, despite their waywardness, God had kept commitment with them. Again and again, God had shown up, shown out and above all God had been the source of power and the foundation of their faith and actions as prophets who spoke in God's name.

That's a gift that we can count on. God is with us, has always been with us, will always be with us, leading us, guiding us, supporting us, delivering us, transforming us into what God desires us to be. Ask the people who would not give in to slavery, who refused to lay down in defeat against Jim Crow laws and the continued devaluation of Black lives. We won't give up, we won't turn back, because the journey to the place of transfiguration of divine-revealing light is God's directive and God walks with us even when there is death and destruction along the way. We will not be sidetracked or turned back even when what waits ahead may mean that we suffer pain and grief. God's presence on the journey gives us strength and the reward of glory is worth every painful step.

In walking with Elijah to the place of his transfiguration, Elisha walks the journey to his own transformation. He sticks with his teacher until he sees him rise to the heavens before his eyes and in the process, he learns that he must now depend fully on God. No longer could he simply stand by his teacher's side, but now without his teacher, but with the Spirit of God moving in him guiding him, anointing him for the task ahead, he is no longer student. He has been transformed, transfigured if you will, for the ministry and the work of the prophet of God. He has become God's mouthpiece.

WOW! Is that what we are called to do? Well, Yes! Change is always difficult. But being changed to reflect the image of God to the people of God is the difficult, the very difficult request that God makes of you, of each one of us who stand in the gap being God's mouthpiece. It's what you must face up to every time you dare to stand before the people of God to preach a word of hope and faith and life in all its fullness. It is what is required of you if you want to be a preacher of the gospel, and by the way that is more than what you do on Sundays or whenever people gather to worship, it is what you are called to do with your whole life.

Recently someone said the "urban legend" (I like the term) is that my class should be avoided at all costs because I am a hard professor. Well, if you come expecting a walk-through that does not challenge you to be faithful in presenting the proclamation of divine grace to the people of God, well then, yes that's a correct description. Because you see what awaits you as the prophet of God is a hard thing. You have responded to a very difficult request, and the decision you have made to help guide God's people in the way of truth and justice is a difficult one, and you had better be prepared for what awaits you. If you are going to stand up for justice, it takes more, much more than blocking traffic one day—as good as that showing was, or even wearing armbands to show that you are advocating for justice for the oppressed and the down-trodden.

That's somewhat easy to do with your friends and colleagues in this safe space. But how do you proclaim justice in the places where you are sent, where that homogeneous community refuses to hear that anyone unlike them is worthy of the same care and consideration? How do you call on people who are guided by the unequal treatment and the unfair and deliberately demeaning portrayals of people of color, Black people in particular, that they see on television to speak out for justice on behalf of "those people?" What do you do when those nearest and dearest to you urge you to turn back from the way that will change who you are in their eyes because you have been transformed, transfigured by the light of God shining in and through you?

Elisha had to wait until he saw Elijah taken up to heaven in order to receive the double portion of spirit he wanted. I'm not sure what that double portion looks like, but I do know that God's Spirit is ready and available; that God's anointing is sure for all who persevere in the task to which God has called them, God anoints us for service in answer to God's call on our lives. The Spirit of God, the anointing Holy Spirit of God transforms our lives. And it is that anointing that enables us to face God's people to keep covenant with God no matter how difficult the task may seem.

Some of you are already working in congregations and have begun to see the challenges that come with pastoral ministry. Hopefully that will inspire you to give your all, to persevere, to learn diligently, to stay the course that has been set before you. And one thing I know for certain is that God anoints and thus transforms us for God's service. So, keep on walking, keep on learning. Stay focused, and experience the anointing, transfiguring grace of God.

Thanks be to God.

A DIVINE DO-OVER

This sermon was preached during the annual spiritual life retreat for members of a large multi-ethnic suburban congregation. There are persons of multiple ages, and years of membership, many of whom have recently become members of the church.

SCRIPTURE TEXT: 2 Corinthians 5:16–21

SERMON STYLE: Journey to Celebration

SERMON PURPOSE STATEMENT: In view of the care and concern about their spiritual life individually and their desire to deepen their life as Christian, I want the people to experience the assurance of God's anointing grace filling them and guiding them through their life, by means of a celebrative sermon on 2 Corinthians 5:16–21 that assures them of their identity as children of God.

GOOD NEWS STATEMENT: Christ reconciles us to God daily so that we can live fully as Children of God.

DISCIPLESHIP MESSAGE STATEMENT: Claim your newness, live into it, become the righteousness of God for the sake of the world.

Introduction

On Monday on Oprah's post–Academy Awards show, Geoffrey Fletcher who received the award for Best Adapted Screenplay for the movie *Precious*, was given a chance for a do-over. He had been so blown away at receiving the award that he could not get the words out to thank the people he wanted to thank, such as Sapphire who wrote the book *Push* that had been adapted to become the movie. On Sunday evening as I read the confirming e-mail, and just knew that the schedule was wrong because I had done nothing to prepare to preach at this service, I hurriedly read the lectionary texts for the upcoming Sunday to see what would fall out. And reading the scripture texts for the third Sunday of Lent, I noted that they were about changes and newness—or a do-over, if you will—for the persons and communities involved.

The concept of Do-Over is not one that I grew up with. My mother drummed into us that first impressions are lasting. She would say, you have only one time to make a first impression, and that needs always to be a good impression—your best impression. And yet as I considered the Bible stories and the theme that seemed to leap out of the pages, I thought, isn't that what the Christian life is? Isn't it our opportunity to do over our lives as children of God?

The Old Testament passage from Joshua 5:9–12 talks about the new way of living for the community that has come into a new land. God instructs them to live into the newness of their situation. And then a much more familiar text, the parable of the Prodigal Son from Luke. There's all kinds of change and newness going on, especially for the younger son, who is given the opportunity to do-over his life. And the one who gives him the opportunity is the same father who he essentially buried according to his culture, by asking for his share of his inheritance before his father died. And as we read this letter from Paul to the Corinthians, that certainly seems to be what he is saying.

Situation/complication

Not in so many words, but the opportunity for a do-over seems to be the crux of Paul's message in this his third letter to the Corinthians. Yes, his third letter because scholars acknowledge that the first one was lost and all we have are some references to it in the first published letter to the Corinthians. Paul wants to impress on this church, that continues to have problems with his leadership, that their life in Christ is a do-over, a divine do-over, initiated by God. Certainly, given the number of problems that he is having with this congregation, Paul is justified in asking them to start over. But that is not where Paul's focus lies. Paul points them to Christ. He reminds them of their identity as Christians. Although he is in a bad situation with respect to his relationship with the people, he calls them to look at him and each other not from their identity as rich or poor, slave or free, male or female, but as new people in Christ. The same one who had proudly spoken of his Jewish heritage, his training and place as a Pharisee, one who had persecuted those who followed Christ, is, I believe very aware, and very thankful that he had been given a do-over by Christ. He understands it for what it is, what it means to his life, what it means to the church, the followers of the Way, and what it could mean to the whole people of God. So, in a simple sentence he tells them, "If anyone is in Christ, there is a new creation, everything old has become new." These are powerful words. In our own situation as disciples of Jesus Christ, do we accept them, do we believe them?

Gospel Assurance to Complication

Do we accept, recognize or live into the newness that Christ's death has given us? Or are we stuck in our sinful human situation, unwilling or unable to see others, or ourselves as persons who have been reconciled with God because of Christ's sacrifice for us? I know that there are some people, some groups who have a problem with the whole notion of sacrifice, I claim it eagerly and unreservedly because it is the source of my newness. I need to claim it, and beyond the whole issue of blood and death, which I agree may be hard to take, I believe we Christians need to claim it because it is only through the sacrificial love of God that we can even hope to accept others or follow the commission of Christ and call others into the fellowship of believers.

In Christ, God was reconciling the world to himself, not counting their trespasses against them, and entrusting the message of reconciliation to us. Do you get it? It is Christology at its best. Jesus Christ the Savior, the Redeemer of the world, whose life was poured out as a libation for us, is the source of our ministry as messengers of God's love for all people, as ambassadors of reconciliation for the world. In other words, until and unless you first receive Christ and accept the gift of new life Christ offers, you cannot hope to help others to know Christ, to bring others into the fellowship of Christ. Paul's message to that early church community, to the church through the ages and to us today, resonates with the promise of divine grace. The words from the Apostle Paul are really Christ's words to us. They speak of the assurance of the favor we enjoy as persons made new through Christ, reclaiming our identity as children of God, made in the image of God, through a do-over initiated by Christ, a divine do-over. However long we have lived, regardless of how young or how old we are, because of our inheritance of human sin, we face the reality that we need the saving grace of Christ to experience life in all its fulness. And the good news is that the reconciling grace of God makes us new every day and enables us to claim our full identity as the redeemed children of God, regardless of where or when we started our Christian journey.

Resolution/Celebration

Most, if not all of us here, hope that in some way, whether as a Christian Educator, Camp Counselor, musician, church leader, elder, deacon, or simply just a sometime worshipper, that your life, your work, your spoken and unspoken witness will lead others to knowledge of and commitment to Christ. It is what drives us when things get rough. It is as the song says, the wind beneath our wings. And the only way that we can hope to do any of the tasks that come with our choice of ministry, is to accept the newness that Christ offers in our own lives. Too often we take it for granted that because we know about Christ, we have accepted Christ and allowed ourselves to be new persons in Christ. Christ took on human form, accepted the magnitude of human sin so that we who follow Christ, can become like Christ in his divine nature, which is the righteousness of God. Let me say it another way: "God so loved the world that God gave Jesus Christ as a do-over for the sin of human beings." It was God who initiated this action. Through the death and resurrection of Jesus, God initiated a do-over for all people. And each of us must make the decision and act on that decision to become a new person through our intentional acceptance of Jesus Christ as lord of our lives. But the most wonderful thing is that we don't even have to make that decision on our own.

Christ reconciles us to God so that we can be made new, so that we can become the person, the people that God intended us to be. And the wonderful thing about this is that it's not a once and done. No, Christ reconciles us to God *daily* so that we can be made new every day, every moment of our lives, so that we can become the person, the people that God always intended us to be, from the moment of creation. It's worth celebrating. Imagine, we are not left on our own to be all that God calls us to be or to do. No matter how far we stray, Christ reconciles us to God so that we are made new, and we can live into the truth of our identity as made in the *imago dei*. In whatever way we are called to be ambassadors for Christ, we can be faithful to our Christian identity and our mission in the world, by allowing the do-over that God has initiated for us through Jesus Christ. It is the reason Christ came to earth; it is the purpose that he died on the cross and rose from the grave; it is the gift that was given to us by a loving creator through our blessed redeemer. Christ reconciles us to God and through him we are made new each day to live fully as redeemed children of God. Through Christ, we can live in righteousness and celebrate the newness that we have in Christ that makes us one with him and with each other.

Conclusion

Oprah's gift of a do-over to Geoffrey Fletcher brought him great joy. He gratefully took advantage of the opportunity to make right his wrongs, or his omissions, and we celebrated the moment and the award with him all over again. God initiated and continues to initiate divine do-overs for us through the presence of Jesus Christ—every day, maybe even every minute. And because of that, each of us is a new creation and that is worth celebrating every day of our lives. The newness that came with our baptism, with our conversion, was our first do-over and that was a time of celebration. And the celebration continues throughout our lives because Jesus Christ offers us unlimited do-overs. Jesus Christ reconciles us to God and through him, we can experience and show forth the righteousness of God in our lives. All we need to do is accept it, step out and live into the newness of Christ. "We entreat you on behalf of Christ, be reconciled to God." Claim your newness, live into it fully, become the righteousness of God for the sake of the world.

THE RAINBOW COVENANT

This sermon was preached for Black History Month at the weekly chapel service for the staff of one of the general agencies of the United Methodist Church committed to justice. The attendees were an eclectic, multi-racial, multicultural group of persons representing multiple levels of personnel.

SCRIPTURE TEXT: Genesis 9:8–17

SERMON STYLE: Biblical Expository with points

SERMON PURPOSE STATEMENT: In view of their commitment to seek freedom and justice for all people, I want the congregation to experience the assurance of God's presence moving them forward as they strive to keep covenant with their stated goal, by means of a biblical expository sermon on Genesis 9:8–17 that speaks of God's presence moving Noah and all people to new things through God's re-creating presence.

GOOD NEWS STATEMENT: God re-creates us daily to live a life of freedom and justice for all people by the saving grace of God.

DISCIPLESHIP MESSAGE STATEMENT: Let us trust in God's grace as we work together for justice for all people.

SERMON POINTS:

Point 1—The story of the flood offers evidence of God's grace to humanity.

Point 2—Despite our sinfulness, God willingly makes covenant with human beings and gives us grace abundantly.

Point 3—God enables us to live righteously with justice for all people only by God's grace.

Introduction

I've always loved rainbows. As someone who was born in a country with two seasons—the rainy season and the dry season—growing up, the sight of a rainbow was not an unusual occurrence. And although I didn't understand the scientific explanation of the rainbow being a phenomenon that is caused by the reflection, or refraction of drops of water and sunlight, its appearance in the sky always made me stop and look. And in doing so, I would always wonder and marvel about the eternal God, who is not only omnipotent and omniscient but also cares about beauty and takes time to offer the glory of nature in flowers and trees, birds and butterflies, in the colors of the sunrise and the sunset and rainbows; and (Oh yes), in people. In the movie *The Color Purple*, two women, Celie and Shug, are having a conversation as they walk in a field of purple flowers. Along the way they talk about God's love of beauty. And Celie asks: Is God vain? Shug says, no, God just doesn't like it when we walk by beautiful things and don't notice them. Rainbows are beautiful and worthy of notice, and more than that.

Body

However you understand this biblical story, whether simply as myth or manufactured story for a beleaguered people, the saving of Noah and his family should give us pause. Scholars describe the flood as an act of divine judgment. God is un-creating the world because of the violence that had corrupted it, or as Old Testament scholar Claus Westermann puts it, the flood is "the archetype of human catastrophe." But in a world, our world, where violence and corruption, where human devaluation and destruction are the order of the day, the story of the flood cannot be simply one of judgment. It is not simply a story about God's total disgust with created humanity. No, God's grace comes through loud and clear and that is where we find ourselves at the location of this biblical text. In fact, the first point that I want to bring to our attention is that *the story of the flood offers evidence of God's grace to humanity.*

At this point in the story, Noah and his immediate family and a remnant of every living creature that God had created, are all standing on dry ground. This is God's plan in action. God is not about destruction. God is about creation and re-creation. God not only saves a remnant, but God also makes covenant with all of creation for all time. God makes an everlasting promise, and signs it with a multi-colored pen. God signs on the dotted line with a rainbow. Did you listen carefully to the text? God is present in the moment of covenant-making. God stands side by side with Noah. God speaks to Noah as friend to friend. There is a personal relationship between God and Noah, and it is solidified in the covenant that speaks of redemption, renewal and above all the amazing, incomparable, eternal grace of God. Yes, some would say Awesome. And you see, that's the wonder and the majesty of this story for us. It is about a God who is more than some far-off power. It speaks of our God, who stands with us making us, and all things, new, every day; and we see the proof in the rainbow.

God's relationship with God's people does not exist in a hands-off, distanced place that results simply and solely in God's judgment being visited on all those who separate themselves from the law of God. If that were so, then the fight to end slavery would not have taken so long, and so many innocent lives would not have been lost. With one flash of lightning, or a thunderbolt worthy of Thor, or perhaps a well-placed tornado or hurricane, God could simply have struck down the perpetrators of such terrible evil. But God's desire is not to bring creation to an end, although God has every reason to do so, because of what we have done with God's creation—nature as well as human beings. In this story, as in all of life, we see the redeeming grace of God present and at work in us and in the world.

There are many important, noteworthy things about this divine action, but one in particular that I want to bring to your attention. Although we act like it, human beings were not the only things that God created to inhabit the earth. In the same way that there are multiple colors in the rainbow, God created multiple types of creatures, above, on, under and in the earth. And God gave us the responsibility to care for the created order. God would not allow the destruction of all of nature; of all the innocent creatures that lived alongside of humanity. No, God took pains to ensure that the world, washed clean, would begin anew with Noah and his family, and all the creatures that God ordained to inhabit the world. The beauty of the rainbow should remind us of the beauty of life that God has ordained for the whole created order. So why then do we as human beings act like it is OK for some of us to claim the world's bounty for ourselves; to decide that freedom and justice are the right of a select few; to act as though nature and all of creation are theirs not simply to enjoy but to abuse; and that includes other human beings that they consider different and therefore inferior? Why is that the order of the day for the society in which we live, and in the world? The rainbow reminds us that God's covenant is with all of creation. It gives witness to the covenant relationship that connects us, human beings, with the God of all creation. Thus, the second point that this text makes for this occasion is that *despite our sinfulness, God willingly makes covenant with human beings and gives us grace abundantly.*

In this text that marks the initiatory act of the divine/human covenant, we see a picture of the creator who loves the creation enough to have a do-over, or maybe the more common term, a make-over, when the original creation goes bad. With this action God sets in motion the act of salvation and deliverance that offers restoration to all creation, and the rainbow that beautifies the sky above us is a visible sign of that grace-filled divine covenant. The evidence is clear in scripture that not only does God decry the evil that humans perpetrate against one another, but also that God suffers along with those who are victimized, and that God's intent is to make all things new—again, and again, and again. That is the nature of God. And in the re-creation that God initiates, is justice. You see that's the real meaning of divine justice.

In the same way as it is God's nature to create; justice is also intrinsic to God. Justice is all about being right with God, living a righteous life, and the only way we can live a life of justice is to open ourselves to God's re-creation of our lives day by day by day. You see, God wants to bring about justice in the world and in all of creation. That's what the rainbow covenant is all about. It is a sign of God's justice and that means judgment that is ruled by compassion and that is grace. Indeed, as Psalm 103 reminds us, God is "gracious, slow to anger and abounding in steadfast love." And in the rainbow covenant, the divine/human covenant, is love and justice for all people.

And since this is Black History Month, I cannot continue without naming the struggle for justice that continues to be a continuing and unresolved issue for Black people in America and sadly, in the church. For me, again sadly, the fruit of the labor expended by our ancestors in the struggle, who fought to claim the benefits of the rainbow covenant that began with Noah, have not been in concert with the efforts that they expended, or even as the seed that they sowed through the sacrifice of their lives. Thousands died, some named and some not, and yet still we are fighting for the benefits of that original covenant—for recognition of our full humanity so that the killing of Black people, especially young Black men does not continue to be a spectator sport; for full voting rights; for an end to the new slave pens that hold generations of young Black men and women incarcerated in jails and prisons all across the USA; for an end to poverty and homelessness in the richest nation in the world, etc., etc., etc. And I wonder when the justice that is ours through the divine covenant, by means of the rainbow covenant God made with Noah for all people, will be allowed to be a reality in our world. When will all the people of God live into the saving, re-creating grace of God? It's a question for us as the church of Jesus Christ.

Although the colors are a little different, ours is a rainbow world. As I said earlier, God likes beauty, that's why we are all different, even though we are all made in the image of God. The rainbow, the sunrise over the sea, the sunset, the trees and flowers and people all originate from God's palette, and the colors, all the colors shine beautifully with the light of God's creative love. No one color is of more value than the other. All are living representations of divine grace, and when it comes to human beings, all are equal in the sight of God. Further, every person stands similarly in need of the grace of God and in fact *it is only by God's grace that we can live righteously and with justice for all people.*

Should not our re-creation, brought about by the waters of our baptism—the sign that we have been re-created, and made new by the saving grace of God—show forth in our lives individually and corporately through our commitment to seek justice for everyone? Should not our acceptance of God's covenant lead us to seek freedom for all people, and thus help to usher in the kin-dom of God? Noah came through the waters of the flood to claim the new life that God had re-created for the world, for all humanity. And through that covenant that reaches to the whole of creation and with the rainbow that represents every tribe and nation under God, visible to all people, we all can claim that heritage, that new life that God has ordained for us. We who have been baptized, Black and White, rich and poor, male and female, gay and straight, young and old, fully abled or physically challenged, English, Spanish, Korean, French, Arab, Portuguese, Chinese, whatever language or culture is native to you, from the hood, the suburbs or deep country, whoever you are, wherever you come from, your heritage and your horizon extends across the rainbow that represents God's abounding love and justice for each and every one of us. God re-creates our lives daily under the terms of that rainbow covenant.

In other words, it is by God's grace that we are able to live a life of justice in the world. God's grace is more than sufficient for our lives. Only by God's grace can we hope to overcome our human inclination to sin, to treat people who are different than we are unjustly and judgmentally. It's amazing how quickly and how readily we are to allow the differences in our human makeup to separate us, to cause us to feel superior without any reason, and to pass judgement on others. But even with all that, Christ does not give up on us. No, by divine grace, we have the opportunity every day, every hour, every minute to show the image of God in our lives and to do justice, love kindness and walk humbly with God. God re-creates us daily in God's image by the unending saving love of God. That's what the rainbow, with its glorious colors is all about. It is the beauty of God's love for us on bold display, reminding us, ensuring us of God's amazing, unending grace.

Conclusion

The everlasting covenant represented in the sign of the rainbow has been ratified by our baptism that is a once-in-a-lifetime sign of our participation in the covenant between God and humanity. That covenant not only reassures us that God will never again destroy the world by flood, but it also assures us that through the water of baptism we have new life; we are re-created to experience oneness with God. That is the clear message of the rainbow. It is the symbol of God's eternal covenant with humanity; God's unending love for us and God's call to us to love one another. It's our heritage; it's our horizon. It's God's promise of God's eternal kin-dom. God re-creates us daily to live a life of freedom and justice for all people.

Let us trust in God's grace as we work together for justice for all people. And may we live in God's covenant now and for all eternity.

FAITHFUL DISCIPLESHIP

This sermon was preached to a suburban congregation that is very diverse racially and culturally. The people are generally middle class economically and take seriously their privileged situation. This is a Reconciling Congregation, with much gender diversity, family groups and singles, with many lay servants active in ministry. The members are politically liberal and actively involved in the political situation in their community and very responsive to requests for support of specific needs. The congregation is committed to ministries for the needy, the homeless, the elderly, substance abusers, and mission at home and abroad. This is a generally healthy congregation, and their most recent stewardship campaign focus is on strengthening their Christian discipleship.

SCRIPTURE TEXTS: Philippians 3:4b–14; Romans 5:1–5

SERMON STYLE: Topical

SERMON PURPOSE STATEMENT: In view of the congregation's commitment to make faithful Christian discipleship their first stewardship goal, I want the congregation to experience the challenge and the reward of responding to the call to faithful living in Christ by means of a topical sermon on faithful discipleship highlighting the empowerment of the Holy Spirit in becoming and living as Christian disciples.

GOOD NEWS STATEMENT: The Holy Spirit empowers us to be faithful disciples of Jesus Christ.

DISCIPLESHIP MESSAGE STATEMENT: Let us strive together to live faithfully as disciples of Jesus Christ.

SERMON POINTS:

Point 1—Each one of us is required to make the decision to be a disciple of Jesus Christ.

Point 2—Living a life that exemplifies faithful discipleship in Christ requires endurance and perseverance in faith.

Point 3—The Holy Spirit gifts us with the perseverance that enables us to be faithful in our Christian discipleship.

Introduction

Back in 2010, just after the winter Olympics, one day while I was at my hairdresser, a young man walked in and came over to Sandy, my hairdresser. When Sandy told me that he was Shani Roberts, Olympic gold medalist in Speed Skating, and gave me the opportunity to meet him, I jumped at the chance. As I chatted with him about his Olympics experience, he shared with me his drive for speed skating and the determination that kept him going. His strategy was to set a goal and go after it, regardless of any obstacle that confronted him. He told me there had been a lot of challenges along the way, but he was determined to be the best speed skater possible and he refused to let anything stop him.

I believe you know that our Olympic Games today is a continuation of the games that were held back in the time of the apostle Paul, and as I considered the decision we have made as a church to give focused attention on faithful discipleship as a key part of our stewardship campaign, both Shani's and Paul's determination came to mind. In his letter to the church at Philippi Paul expresses his determination to persevere in order to reach his ultimate goal of being a faithful follower of Jesus Christ.

Body

Point 1—It almost goes without saying that in order to follow Christ faithfully, we must persevere in our faith. But before we can take the steps or make the hard decisions that are often necessary in our Christian walk, there is an initial step that is required. Paul came to faith in Christ after he was stopped in his tracks on the Damascus Road, but while he lay sightless, he had the opportunity to make the decision to follow Christ. Many, if not most of us do not have such a dramatic encounter, but *each one of us is required to make the decision to be a disciple of Jesus Christ.* Our baptism makes us a member of the body of Christ and for those of us baptized as infants, confirmation is evidence of that decision. Although one would think that our baptism or confirmation guarantees faithful Christian living, the reality is that following Christ faithfully is not that simple. In a world and a society marked by injustice in so many ways, being a faithful disciple of Jesus Christ means taking on the stance of compassion and humility at times when the world and our human mind encourages us to do just the opposite. One is required each day, perhaps each minute or each second to make decisions about one's life that are in accord with what Jesus requires of us.

As Christians we are called to show the same humility and compassion that Christ exemplified in his life on earth. Christ in his saving love opened for us the way to God that we had lost through human sinfulness, and through his forgiving grace we can find our way to God. But doing so calls us to make choices in life that are often difficult and contrary to what the world encourages us to do. Being a faithful disciple of Christ is often a test of our faith that calls for perseverance.

Point 2—We are called as followers of Christ to do the hard work of loving those who act in ways that are unlovely, and that is no easy task. As disciples of Jesus Christ, our life must give witness to our love of God and neighbor totally as Christ requires. But the truth of the matter is that *living a life that exemplifies faithful Christian living requires endurance and perseverance.* The truth of the matter is that Christian discipleship and perseverance in faith go hand in hand. To persevere means to remain steadfast on whatever course one has taken, despite any difficulty that may come in one's way. It means to refuse to be deterred from whatever path one has decided to pursue. The apostle Paul is a worthy example of one who persevered in the face of major odds, to live out his ministry as a follower of Jesus Christ. In his letter to the Philippians, he speaks of the importance of living into the call to Christian discipleship. His ultimate goal is life with Christ for all eternity, and Paul wants us to hear that in order for him to reach that goal, he has to keep pressing on; to persist; to persevere; to keep his eyes on the prize of the "heavenly call of God in Christ Jesus." Despite the beatings, imprisonment, shipwrecks, Paul continued day by day to live into that commitment. And each of us is also called to live into our commitment each day of our lives, so that our work and our witness exemplify our Christian discipleship.

The fledgling Christian churches of the New Testament were subject to many kinds of persecution, but they persevered because of their belief in Jesus Christ. In his letter to the Romans, to a people he hoped to meet, Paul writes a word of encouragement to help them, and ultimately us, as disciples, to stay the course on which they were set, a course that leads to eternity with Christ. He assures them of the peace that is theirs because of their faith in Christ; that he believed would enable them to endure the trials they experienced as their lives were transformed by their faith in Christ.

Point 3—But none of us can maintain our discipleship faithfully without the grace of God that is given to us by the Holy Spirit. We can keep on keeping on only through the power of the Holy Spirit. Said another way, *faithfulness in our Christian discipleship is a gift of grace through the Holy Spirit.* In Ephesians 2:8 Paul tells us: "For by grace you have been saved through faith, and that is not our own doing, it is the gift of God." And that is a message for us as we commit to taking on the challenge of faithful Christian discipleship as critical to our stewardship.

In the past, we have tried to be faithful in living out the mandate of Christ to care for our neighbors through many ministries of care. Our PADS ministry that provides safe sleeping space and care to many who are homeless, our ministry to the elderly, our mission trips, and our intentional outreach to families in need, our commitment to justice for our LGBTQ siblings tell our story. And yet, as we have taken inventory of our spiritual lives, we believe that something is missing. So here we are, wanting to draw closer to Christ and to live individually and together a life that shows our maturity as disciples of Jesus Christ.

In all of life there are challenges to our faith—challenges to our stance that is unpopular with some people—but when we follow Christ faithfully, we can be assured that Christ supports us through the Holy Spirit that pours the love of God into our hearts, enabling us to face all challenges. The Holy Spirit gives us the strength to endure life's trials so we can press on, toward our goal of faithful discipleship in Christ. In other words, *the Holy Spirit empowers us to be faithful disciples of Jesus Christ.*

Conclusion

By grace Paul endured and persevered to reach his goal and we can also. If as Paul says we "want to know Christ and the power of his resurrection" we cannot waffle and waver, we must be faithful and persistent in our witness as Christians. Through the Holy Spirit we experience the joy and peace in our souls that testifies to the grace of God supporting us on our journey as Christian disciples.

In our conversation, Shani told me his true goal was not simply to win gold at the Olympics. Oh, yes, that was a goal, and he met it in 2006, but his ultimate goal was to be the best speed skater he could be. Our goal must be to be faithful followers of Christ in all aspects of our lives. And we can meet that goal through the power of the Holy Spirit. So, my sisters and brothers, *let us strive together to reach our goal and live faithfully as Christians, true followers of Jesus Christ.*

APPENDIX A
Guidelines for Homiletical Exegesis for Good News Sermons

A. Analysis of the Context

- What is the congregational context in which the sermon will be preached? What are the social, cultural, theological, and doctrinal norms?
- Consider their current situation and specifically, what they are feeling or experiencing, individually or as a congregation.
- Establish the boundaries of the preaching context: liturgical or social implications, societal or world events.
- Approach the situation of preaching with the understanding that the congregation has the expectation of hearing good news.
- Connect context with text: Is there special significance to the context that has implications for the meaning of the text?
- Determine the appropriateness of the good news: How can the message of the text be transformative for the individual hearers or for the congregation?

B. Identifying the Good News

- Approach the text or topic with prayerful expectation of finding good news.

- Find the theological meaning: What does the text or topic say about God and the divine/human relationship?
- Name the good news: Identify the divine action that speaks of human transformation.
- Identify a charge to the hearers that is fueled by the good news.

C. Interpreting the Biblical Test or the Topic

- Meet the text or topic: Approach with the intention of uncovering good news.
- Locate the text biblically. Establish the boundaries of the text: Is there special significance to its placement? Are there bridge words that move the message of the text?
- Locate the text historically: What is the historical setting, that is, the social, religious, cultural, (etc.) realities that confront or are confronted by the text in its original setting? How did the text function in and affect the lives of those who heard it first?
- Identify the literary form of the text and its influence on the reading of the text. Does the form offer a model for the sermon? Engage your senses and your imagination as you immerse yourself in the contents of the text.
- Consider the theological implications of the text: What is its influence on Christian doctrine or practice? How is it supported biblically?
- Depending on the style of sermon, connect text or topic and identify biblical and theological agreements or differences.

APPENDIX B
Guidelines for Homiletical Exegesis for a Biblical Expository Sermon

A. Define the Preaching Context

- What is the social, cultural, theological and doctrinal situation of the preaching context?
- What are the demographics and the congregational context in which the sermon will be preached?
- What current issues in the life of the congregation need to be addressed?
- Identify broader social, cultural and economic issues in the wider community beyond the immediate congregation that need to be addressed.
- What are the societal, cultural, political, or other issues nationally and globally that need to be considered in the development of the sermon?

B. Meet the Text

- What immediate personal, pastoral, and social concerns and expectations do you bring with *you* to the text?
- How many times have you read the passage, and which different versions have you read? What meaningful differences did you find in the reading of different translations?

- What new insights arise from your reading of the text?
- What is fresh and new to you in this reading of the text as you consider the context in which it will be preached?
- What are your initial impressions, questions, and sermon ideas?

C. LOCATE THE TEXT BIBLICALLY

- Where is the selected text is placed within the particular book?
- What events come before and after those in your text?
- Is there a reason why the passage is placed where it is? Is there special significance to its placement?
- How does this passage function in the overall contents of the particular biblical book?

D. LOCATE THE TEXT HISTORICALLY

- Who was the author of the text? What is the level of authorship? - i.e. historical event, oral tradition, redaction.
- Where, when, and why was the text written?
- What is the history *behind the text*? In what historical situation was the text developed? How much of that historical context is relevant to your sermon?
- What is the history *within the text*? What are the social, religious, and cultural realities that confront or are confronted by the text in this setting?
- How did the text function in and affect the lives of those who heard it first?

E. ENGAGE THE LITERARY CONTENTS OF THE TEXT:

- Is the literary form of the text identifiable as narrative/non-narrative, saga, myth, legend, historical narrative, scholastic writing, dialogue, parable, etc.?
- How does the literary form influence your reading of the text?
- Are there specific bridge words that move the message of the text? How and where do they lead you in your engagement of the text?

- Which words have history that bears examination or have greatest relevance for the present reality? Why?
- Does the literary form of the text offer a model for the sermon? If so, identify it.

F. Engage Your Senses and Emotions in the Text

- What do you see, hear, smell, taste and touch as you read the text?
- What emotions do you experience as you read the text?
- Having immersed yourself in the text as a biblical, historical, and literary document, how do you think it felt to be one of the first hearers of the text in that situation?
- Use your imagination to connect the text with contemporary or historical art, events, literature, nature, people, or other elements that allow you to connect the text with the present. Identify at least three elements that help to bring the text to life.

G. Theologically Interpret the Text in the Congregational Context

- What attributes of God does this text provide for you?
- How does this text help to inform your understanding of the divine/human relationship?
- What theological topics or themes arise or could be developed from the text in light of the preaching context?
- Are there parallels to be made between the context of the text and the current situation of the congregation?

H. Identify Good News in the Text for the Present

- What evidence of divine grace found in the text can offer good news to the present congregation?
- How does this good news lead to a call to discipleship?
- How can the message of the text be transformative for the current situation of the congregation?

APPENDIX C
Guidelines for Homiletical Exegesis for a Topical Sermon

A. Define the Preaching Context

- What is the social, cultural, theological and doctrinal situation of the preaching context?
- What are the demographics and the congregational context in which the sermon will be preached?
- What current issues in the life of the congregation need to be addressed?
- Identify broader social, cultural and economic issues beyond the immediate congregation that need to be addressed.
- What are the societal, political, world or other issues that need to be considered in the development of the sermon?

B. Meet the topic

- What is the specific topic you are preaching?
- What is the perceived congregational need that originated this topic?
- How does this topic connect with the congregational need you have determined i.e. how does preaching on this topic engage the response to the need you have selected?

- Is this topic connected with a Christian doctrine, tradition, or practice?
- What is your understanding of the meaning of this topic?
- What are the key points you wish to make that exposes and connects the topic to the congregation?

C. CONNECT THE TOPIC WITH A FOUNDATION OF SCRIPTURE

- What scripture text have you selected as foundational to the topic?
- What is the historical setting and how much of it does your sermon require?
- What are the social, religious, cultural, etc. realities that confront or are confronted by the text in its original setting?
- Having immersed yourself in the historical event, how do you think it felt to be in that situation?
- What is the form of the text and how does the form influence your reading of the text?

D. EXPANDING THE SCRIPTURAL BASE OF THE TOPIC

- What are two or three additional texts that are supportive to the topic and related to the foundational text?
- How do these texts connect with the foundational text?
- In what way does the representation of the topic in those texts match the way it appears in the foundational text?
- What are the commonalities of meaning, culture, historicity and application to the biblical contexts?

E. LOCATE THE TOPIC THEOLOGICALLY AND DOCTRINALLY

- How has the topic been understood and interpreted theologically?
- What scriptures and interpretations have commonly been used in preaching this topic?
- How has the topic been applied in general or denominational Christian doctrines, traditions or practices?

- What is the common understanding (if any) of the topic in the present congregation?
- Does your approach fit or counter their understanding of the topic?

F. LOCATE THE TOPIC HISTORICALLY AND CONTEXTUALLY

- How has this topic been approached historically in the wider church?
- What, if any, misunderstandings has the preaching of this topic caused previously?
- Is there a situation present in the society or the world for which this topic has particular relevance?

G. MEET THE CONGREGATION

- What does this topic say to or about this congregation?
- Is there a reason or situation past or present why the congregation will resist hearing this topic preached?
- Does the presentation of the topic lend itself to offering good news to the hearers?
- Why have you taken the particular approach to addressing the topic?

H. SIGNIFICANCE OF THE TOPIC FOR THE PRESENT

- Why do you think your approach to this topic will achieve significance for the present congregation?
- What good news from scripture relates to the application of this topic in the congregation?
- How does the discipleship message of the sermon connect and relate to the topic?

APPENDIX D
Weekly Schedule for Sermon Preparation

MONDAY: READ THE TEXT AND IDENTIFY THE PURPOSE OF THE SERMON

- Read the chosen scripture text as part of your early morning devotions.
- Read the full pericope and surrounding text as you are led in your reading.
- Listen carefully for the message of divine grace that arises from the text.
- Create a Sermon Purpose Statement as a guide to focus your sermon development.
- Determine the style of sermon you will preach and if topical, consider the appropriateness of the topic to the text.

TUESDAY: READ AND EXEGETE THE TEXT

- Read the text as part of your morning devotions. Read multiple translations if possible.
- Guided by the Sermon Purpose Statement, create the Good News and Discipleship Message Statements.
- Consider the style of sermon you will develop.

- Begin the initial work of biblical interpretation through research and data gathering.

Wednesday: Frame the Sermon

- Complete the research and any remaining exegetical work.
- Develop an outline based on the style or intended shape of the sermon.
- Consider the movement and transitions necessary to connect the text with the congregational context in which the sermon will be preached.
- Give careful attention to the content of Introduction and the closing message or conclusion.

Thursday: Prepare the Sermon Manuscript

- Using the completed outline, create the sermon manuscript.
- Compare the contents of the sermon with the Sermon Purpose Statement.
- Verify or modify the Good News and Discipleship Message Statements in the manuscript.
- Allow the material of the sermon to permeate the mind and the heart.

Friday: Read, Review, Revise, Reformulate

- Read the manuscript carefully, engaging all your senses in verifying its contents.
- Review the contents with respect to text or topic and preaching context.
- Pay special attention to transitions between the major sections and functionality of the introduction and conclusion.
- Verify that the Good News is clearly presented and recognizable in the full contents of the sermon.
- Ensure that the message of Christian discipleship is clear and appropriate to the congregational context.

- Make revisions and practice reading the sermon aloud, preferably before a mirror.
- Create notes for preaching (if applicable).

SATURDAY: REREAD, ABSORB THE MESSAGE, AND RELAX

- Review all aspects of the sermon.
- Practice preaching the sermon (before a mirror adds value to the exercise).
- Relax and allow the message to take root in your spirit.

SUNDAY: PREACH THE SERMON AND LET IT GO

- Saturate the sermon in prayer.
- Leave room for the Holy Spirit.
- Preach the sermon.
- Let it go—avoid rehashing.
- Relax.

APPENDIX E
Preaching Feedback Form

Did you hear good news in this sermon? ☐ Yes ☐ No

What was it? ____

____

____

Did you hear a distinct message from this sermon? ☐ Yes ☐ No

What was it? ____

____

____

Did you hear anything that related to your discipleship? ☐ Yes ☐ No

What was it? ____

____

____

Did the scriptures come through clearly? ☐ Yes ☐ No

Which passage(s)? ______________________________

____

____

Did this sermon tell you anything about God? ☐ Yes ☐ No

What was it? ______________________________

____

____

Did the sermon hold your attention? ☐ Yes ☐ No

If yes, how? If no, why not? ______________________________

____

____

Did this sermon relate well to this congregation? ☐ Yes ☐ No

Why or why not? ______________________________

____

____

NOTES

PREFACE

1. Samuel D. Proctor, *The Certain Sound of the Trumpet: Crafting a Sermon of Authority* (Valley Forge, Pa.: Judson Press, 1994), 12.

2. Ronald J. Allen, *Preaching: An Essential Guide* (Nashville: Abingdon Press, 2002), 20. Allen devotes his first chapter to the subject of good news as it arises from the text and is interpreted as the Word of God. He addresses the subject further in his treatment of contextualizing the sermon for the congregation.

CHAPTER ONE

1. Marjorie Hewitt Suchocki, *The Whispered Word: A Theology of Preaching* (St. Louis: Chalice Press, 1999), 2. Suchocki is a process theologian, who recognizes God as "everlastingly creative, continually calling existence into being through an evocative word."

2. Although the phrase "going on to perfection" has been attributed to the theology of John Wesley, Paul's letter to the Philippians (3:14) offers these sentiments, even more definitively, of continual striving to reach the goal of becoming like Christ.

3. Wesley's preventing grace is more commonly referred to as prevenient grace. It is defined as grace that runs ahead of our desires.

4. Allen, *Preaching: An Essential Guide*, 21. Allen suggests that the preacher summarize the main idea of the sermon with God as subject, the activity of God as the verb, and the predicate as the result of God's redeeming

activity. He believes that "by making God the subject of this sentence, and the subject of the sermon, preachers remind themselves and the congregation of the centrality of God in the Christian worldview, and of the fact that God's gracious initiatives make possible (and call forth) human response."

5. Edmund A. Steimle, Morris J. Niedenthal, and Charles L. Rice, *Preaching the Story* (Philadelphia: Fortress Press, 1980), 38.

6. Ibid.

7. David Buttrick, *Homiletics: Moves and Structures* (Philadelphia: Fortress Press, 1987), 451.

8. Fred B. Craddock, *Preaching* (Nashville: Abingdon Press, 1985), 51–52.

9. Suchocki, *The Whispered Word*, 4.

10. Suchocki warns that the whispered word of God, always a creative word, "can be drowned out by the sheer weight of the past with which and through which it must work (6) [and is] not always clearly discerned" (13).

11. James Forbes, *The Holy Spirit & Preaching* (Nashville: Abingdon Press, 1989), 19.

12. Ibid., 26.

13. Frank A. Thomas, *They Like to Never Quit Praisin' God: The Role of Celebration in Preaching* (Cleveland: Pilgrim Press, 1997). Thomas' work was a continuation of Henry H. Mitchell's thesis developed in his textbook *Celebration & Experience in Preaching* (Nashville: Abingdon Press, 1990).

14. Ibid., 23.

CHAPTER TWO

1. Eugene L. Lowry, *The Sermon: Dancing the Edge of Mystery* (Nashville: Abingdon Press, 1997), 37.

2. John S. McClure, *Preaching Words: 144 Key Terms in Homiletics* (Louisville: Westminster John Knox Press, 2007), 30–31.

3. Ronald J. Allen, *Preaching the Topical Sermon* (Louisville: Westminster John Knox Press, 1992), 35. In chapter 2, Allen lists several occasions and associated conditions connected with preaching the topical sermon.

4. Ronald J. Allen, *Contemporary Biblical Interpretation for Preaching* (Valley Forge, Pa.: Judson Press, 1984), 3. Allen considers the knowledge of the history of the text as facilitating the emergence of the "ancient dimensions of meaning which are not obvious to the modern eye."

5. Allen, *Preaching: An Essential Guide*, 30.

6. Much of the following descriptive material on these interpretive methods was paraphrased and simplified from various articles about biblical hermeneutics, biblical exegesis, and biblical criticism, including defintions provided by www.wikipedia.com.

7. Most of this interpretive material is taken from: *The New Interpreter's Bible: A Commentary in Twelve Volumes* (Nashville: Abingdon Press, 1994–1998.)

8. For more detailed information on biblical exegesis in connection with preaching, in addition to the text referenced previously in this chapter, see Ronald J. Allen, *Interpreting the Gospel* (St. Louis: Chalice Press, 1998); Thomas G. Long, *Preaching and the Literary Forms of the Bible* (Philadelphia: Fortress Press, 1989); David L. Bartlett, *Between the Bible and the Church: New Methods for Biblical Preaching* (Nashville: Abingdon Press, 1999).

CHAPTER THREE

1. John Vincent directed the Sheffield Inner City Ecumenical Mission and the Urban Theology Unit in Sheffield, England. His book *Into the City* (London: Epworth Press, 1982) "tells of the successes and failures of a group of churches and their members who actually live in the inner city, continuing a Christian witness in old and often unsuitable buildings, working alongside underprivileged immigrants and unemployed in areas whose needs have been ignored and forgotten."

2. Fred B. Craddock, *As One without Authority* (St. Louis: Chalice Press, 2001), 18.

3. Paul Scott Wilson, "Theological Reasons for a Change," in *The Four Pages of the Sermon: A Guide to Biblical Preaching* (Nashville: Abingdon Press, 1999), 20–25. Wilson's Four Page model presents the sermon as four theological pages, two of which present the text as stated in scripture; he connects the biblical record with the preaching context through two parallel theological pages.

4. Ibid., 20.

5. From Paul Scott Wilson, "Biblical Studies and Preaching: A Growing Divide?" in Thomas G. Long and Edward Farley, eds., *Preaching as a Theological Task: World Gospel, Scripture. In Honor of David Buttrick* (Louisville: Westminster John Knox Press, 1996), 137. In this book, fifteen homileti-

cians/theologians pay homage by addressing a topic of interest or concern to Buttrick. Wilson's offering addresses specifically the connection between theology and scripture.

6. Ibid., 139. The problem is one that Wilson considers to have been inherited from an older model of preaching that does not fit the present.

7. David Schnasa Jacobsen, *Homiletical Theology in Action: The Unfinished Theological Task of Preaching*, (Eugene, Oregon: Cascade Books, 2015), 1.

8. Ibid.

9. Ibid, v–vi.

CHAPTER FOUR

1. O. Wesley Allen, *The Homiletic of ALL Believers: A Conversational Approach* (Louisville: Westminster John Knox Press, 2005), 17. Allen expounds on the requirements and the difficulties of engaging and maintaining these conversations over time, but stresses their importance in the life of the church. He has developed a Matrix of Conversations, which consists of six levels of conversation with the pulpit at the center of the highest level, overlaid on the liturgical conversation that sits on the simultaneous sociohistorical, personal, theological, and congregational conversations.

2. Thomas, *They Like to Never Quit Praisin' God*, 3.

3. Suchocki, *The Whispered Word*, 3. In the language of the process theologian, God is constantly calling all worlds into being through the never ending Word of God. "To exist is, by definition, to be receiving a word from God."

CHAPTER FIVE

1. For descriptions and examples of thirty-four different types of sermons, see Ronald J. Allen, *Patterns of Preaching: A Sermon Sampler* (St. Louis: Chalice Press, 1998).

2. Long, *Preaching and the Literary Forms of the Bible*, 138–48. Long provides an extensive description and several examples of this process of developing the outline of the sermon.

3. Eugene Lowry, *The Sermon: Dancing the Edge of Mystery* (Nashville: Abingdon Press, 1997), 23.

4. Thomas, *They Like to Never Quit Praisin' God*, 87–89. Thomas charts a process that moves from "Intuitive Complication" through "Intuitive Gospel Assurance" to "Intuitive Celebration," which works as an influence on the emotive behavior of the congregation.

5. Ibid., 88.

6. The Four Pages of the Sermon is a style of sermon developed by Paul Scott Wilson and is explained in a textbook by the same name (Nashville: Abingdon Press, 1999). Wilson considers this style appropriate for all biblical (expository) sermons.

CHAPTER SIX

1. Thomas G. Long, in *God's Word and Our Words: Basic Homiletics* by Ronald E. Sleeth (Atlanta: John Knox Press, 1986), vii.

2. Ronald E. Sleeth, *God's Word and Our Words: Basic Homiletics* (Atlanta: John Knox Press, 1986), 7.

3. Lucy Lind Hogan, *Graceful Speech: An Invitation to Preaching* (Louisville: Westminster John Knox Press, 2006), 147.

4. Lucy Atkinson Rose, *Sharing the Word: Preaching in the Roundtable Church* (Louisville: Westminster John Knox Press, 1997), iii. Rose points out that "in conversational views of preaching, sermonic forms seek to engage the community of faith in its central, ongoing conversations."

5. O. Wesley Allen Jr., *The Homiletic of ALL Believers*, 13.

6. Suchocki, *The Whispered Word*, 4.

7. Richard Lischer, "Preaching as the Church's Language," in *Listening to the Word*, edited by Gail R. O'Day and Thomas G. Long (Nashville: Abingdon Press, 1993), 125.

8. Suchocki, *The Whispered Word*, 11.

9. Charles Rice, *The Embodied Word: Preaching as Art and Liturgy* (Minneapolis: Augsburg Fortress, 1991), 51.

10. Ibid., 25.

BIBLIOGRAPHY

Aden, LeRoy H., and Robert G. Hughes. *Preaching God's Compassion*. Minneapolis: Fortress Press, 2002.

Allen, O. Wesley. *The Homiletic of ALL Believers: A Conversational Approach*. Louisville: Westminster John Knox Press, 2005.

Allen, Ronald J. *Contemporary Biblical Interpretation for Preaching*. Valley Forge, Pa.: Judson Press, 1984.

———. *Hearing the Sermon: Relationship/Content/Feeling*. St. Louis: Chalice Press, 2004.

———. *Interpreting the Gospel*. St. Louis: Chalice Press, 1998.

———. *Preaching: An Essential Guide*. (Nashville: Abingdon Press, 2002.

———. *Preaching the Topical Sermon*. Louisville: Westminster John Knox Press, 1992.

———. *Thinking Theologically*. Minneapolis: Fortress Press, 2008

Allen, Ronald J., and Gilbert L. Bartholomew. *Preaching Verse by Verse*. Louisville: Westminster John Knox Press, 2000.

Allen, Ronald J., and Clark M. Williamson. *Preaching the Gospels without Blaming the Jews: A Lectionary Commentary*. Louisville: Westminster John Knox Press, 2004.

———. *Preaching the Old Testament: A Lectionary Commentary*. Louisville: Westminster John Knox Press, 2007.

Bartlett, David L. *Between the Bible and the Church: New Methods for Biblical Preaching*. Nashville: Abingdon Press, 1999.

Brown, Teresa L.. *Delivering the Sermon*. Minneapolis: Fortress Press, 2008.

Buttrick, David. *Homiletics: Moves and Structures*. Philadelphia: Fortress Press, 1987.

Cosgrove, Charles H., and Edgerton W. Dow. *In other Words Incarnational Translation for Preaching*. Grand Rapids: William B. Eerdmans, 2007.

Craddock, Fred B. *As One without Authority: Revised and with New Sermons*. St. Louis: Chalice Press, 2001.

_________. *Preaching*. Nashville: Abingdon Press, 1985.

Forbes, James. *The Holy Spirit and Preaching*. Nashville: Abingdon Press, 1989.

Gilbert, Kenyatta. *A Pursued Justice: Black Preaching from the Great Migration to Civil Rights*. Grand Rapids: Baylor, 2016.

Greenhaw, David M., and Ronald J. Allen, editors. *Preaching in the Context of Worship*. St. Louis: Chalice Press, 2000.

Harris, James Henry. *Beyond the Tyranny of the Text: Preaching in Front of the Bible to Create a New World*. Nashville: Abingdon Press, 2019.

Hogan, Lucy Lind. *Graceful Speech: An Invitation to Preaching*. Louisville: Westminster John Knox Press, 2006.

Holbert, John and Alyce McKenzie. *What Not to Say: Avoiding the Common Mistakes That Can Sink Your Sermon*. Louisville: Westminster / John Knox Press, 2011.

Jeter, Joseph R., and Ronald J. Allen. *One Gospel, Many Ears: Preaching for Different Listeners in the Congregation*. St. Louis: Chalice Press, 2002.

Kalas, J. Ellsworth. *Preaching in An Age of Distraction*. Downers Grove, Illinois: IVP Books, 2014.

Kay, James F. *Preaching and Theology*. St. Louis: Chalice Press, 2007.

Kim, Eunjoo. *Preaching in An Age of Globalization*. Westminster / John Knox Press, 2010.

LaRue, Cleophus J. *Rethinking Celebration*. Louisville: Westminster John Knox Press, 2016.

Long, Thomas G. *Preaching and the Literary Forms of the Bible*. Philadelphia: Fortress Press, 1989.

_________. *The Witness of Preaching*. Second edition. Louisville: Westminster John Knox Press, 2005.

Lowry, Eugene L. *The Homiletical Plot: The Sermon as Narrative Art Form*. Revised edition. Louisville: Westminster John Knox Press, 2001.

_________. *How to Preach a Parable: Designs for Narrative Sermons*. Nashville: Abingdon Press, 1989.

_________. *The Sermon: Dancing the Edge of Mystery*. Nashville: Abingdon Press, 1997.

McClure, John S. *Preaching Words: 144 Key Terms in Homiletics*. Louisville: Westminster John Knox Press, 2007.

McClure, John S., Ronald J. Allen, Dale P. Andrews, L. Susan Bond, Dan P. Moseley, and G. Lee Ramsey Jr. *Listening to Listeners: Homiletical Case Studies*. St. Louis: Chalice Press, 2004.

McMickle, Marvin A. *Living Water for Thirsty Souls: Unleashing the Power of Exegetical Preaching*. Valley Forge, Pa.: Judson Press, 2001.

Mulligan, Mary Alice, Diane Turner-Sharazz, Dawn Ottoni Wilhelm, and Ronald J. Allen. *Believing in Preaching: What Listeners Hear in Sermons.* St. Louis: Chalice Press, 2005.

Pasquarello, Michael, III. *Christian Preaching: A Trinitarian Theology of Proclamation*. Grand Rapids: Baker Academic, 2006.

Proctor., Samuel D. *The Certain Sound of the Trumpet: Crafting a Sermon of Authority*. Valley Forge, Pa.: Judson Press, 1994.

Rice, Charles. *The Embodied Word: Preaching as Art and Liturgy*. Minneapolis: Augsburg Fortress, 1991.

Rose, Lucy Atkinson. *Sharing the Word: Preaching in the Roundtable Church.* Louisville: Westminster John Knox Press, 1997.

Sleeth, Ronald E. *God's Word and Our Words: Basic Homiletics.* Atlanta: John Knox Press, 1986.

Steimle, Edmund A., Morris J. Niedenthal, and Charles L. Rice. *Preaching the Story*. Philadelphia: Fortress Press, 1980.

Suchocki, Marjorie Hewitt. *The Whispered Word: A Theology of Preaching*. St. Louis: Chalice Press, 1999.

Thomas, Frank A. *They Like to Never Quit Praisin' God: The Role of Celebration in Preaching*. Cleveland: United Church Press, 1997.

Thompson, Lisa L. *Ingenuity: Preaching as an Outsider*. Nashville: Abingdon Press, 2018.

Tisdale, Leonora Tubbs. *Preaching as Local Theology and Folk Art.* Minneapolis: Fortress Press, 1997.

Ward, Richard F. *Speaking of the Holy: The Art of Communication in Preaching.* St. Louis: Chalice Press, 2001.

Webb, Stephen H. *The Divine Voice: Christian Proclamation and the Theology of Sound.* Grand Rapids: Brazos Press, 2004.

Wilson, Paul Scott. *The Four Pages of the Sermon: A Guide to Biblical Preaching*. Nashville: Abingdon Press, 1999.

———. *God Sense: Reading the Bible for Preaching.* Nashville: Abingdon Press, 2001.

Wisdom, Andrew Carl. *Preaching to a Multi-generational Assembly*. Collegeville, Minn.: Liturgical Press, 2004.

Wiseman, Karyn L. *I Refuse to Preach a Boring Sermon: Engaging the 21st Century Listener*. Cleveland, Ohio: Pilgrim Press, 2013.

INDEX